Remembrances of Spring

Lotus Poetry Series
Naomi Long Madgett, Senior Editor

Remembrances of Spring

Collected Early Poems

by

Naomi Long Madgett

Michigan State University Press
East Lansing
1993

Copyright © 1993 by Naomi Long Madgett

All Michigan State University Press Books are produced on paper which
meets the requirements of American National Standard of Information
Sciences—Permanence of paper for printed materials ANSI Z39.48-1984.

Michigan State University Press
East Lansing, MI 48823-5202

Printed in the United States of America

00 99 98 97 96 95 94 93   1 2 3 4 5 6 7 8 9

ISBN 87013-345-4

Library of Congress Cataloging-in-Publication Data

Madgett, Naomi Cornelia Long.
    Remembrances of spring : collected early poems / by Naomi Long
Madgett.
        p.   cm.— (Lotus poetry series ; 1)
        ISBN 0-87013-345-4
        I. Title. II. Series.
PS3525.A318R45   1993
811'.54—dc20
                                                                    93-34603
                                                                    CIP

POETRY BY NAOMI LONG MADGETT

Songs to a Phantom Nightingale (1941)
One and the Many (1956)
Star by Star (1965, 1970)
Pink Ladies in the Afternoon (1972, 1990)
Exits and Entrances (1978)
Phantom Nightingale: Juvenilia (1981)
Octavia and Other Poems (1988)
Remembrances of Spring (1993)

EDITED COLLECTIONS

A Milestone Sampler: 15th Anniversary Anthology (1988)
Adam of Ifé: Black Women in Praise of Black Men (1992)

CONTENTS

One and the Many

PREFACE

I.

Most poets who have achieved some degree of recognition for their mature work would probably shudder at the suggestion that they subject to public scrutiny their precocious childhood efforts. I might have joined them in willing my early scribblings to oblivion had it not been for the fact that they had already become a matter of record before I had the opportunity to exercise an adult choice in the matter.

When *Songs to a Phantom Nightingale* was published in 1941, I had just graduated from high school and my eighteenth birthday was still about two weeks away. I was the same age as Phillis Wheatley was in 1770 when her first poem was published, to be followed by her book three years later. Margaret Walker was about twenty-six years old, looking forward to the publication of *For My People* in 1942. Gwendolyn Brooks, then about twenty-four, was probably still working on *A Street in Bronzeville*, which would appear in 1945. While my small collection did not possess the maturity of those that followed and attracted little attention, the very fact of its existence may nevertheless be of some value among literary historians. While Lucy Terry's crude rhyme, "Bars Fight" (1746), would win no laurels as literary art, it has been recognized traditionally as the historical beginning of recorded African American poetry.

The significance of my little volume did not fully occur to me until, in 1980, Dexter Fisher mentioned it in her introduction to *The Third Woman: Minority Women Writers in the United States* as the beginning of a thirty-year period of poetry by African American women.

Subsequently—and because the first book represented only a very small sampling of my early work—*Phantom Nightingale: Juvenilia* was published in 1981 in order to put on record a number of additional poems written before, during, and for two years after the period covered by the first publication.

That both of these volumes have attracted some critical interest is evident in the essay by Robert Sedlack in the *Dictionary of Literary Biography* (Volume 76), and they are the subject of some discussion in several other studies now in progress or awaiting publication. An increasing number of requests from scholars for copies of my out-of-print poems leads me to believe that there is a need for *Remembrances of Spring*.

Another reason for presenting this material is that it may be helpful in the correction of some erroneous assumptions about dates of composition. One might assume, for example, that my 1941 publication represents the best of the writing of my high school years, but that is not the case. Most of the poems included were written from seventh grade through tenth. There was about a two-year lag while Pegasus Publishing Company, with whom my father had signed a contract, was taken over by Fortuny's, Inc. As I recall, no more than three poems were added to the original manuscript before publication so that many of those written during the interim were omitted. Within another year or so, Fortuny's, too, suffered financial difficulties which resulted in a declaration of bankruptcy.

My little clothbound book, however, did not contribute to the publisher's demise. Priced at one dollar, it justified its existence through fairly good sales. My father, the Rev. Dr. Clarence M. Long, Sr., had made ample use of his wide network of friends and colleagues, especially in the black Baptist churches across the nation, and even now occasional copies turn up in surprising places, including a few university libraries.

According to my dictionary, a nightingale is "a small, Old World migratory bird noted for its melodious nocturnal song." In all my travels I have yet to see or hear one, but its name in the title of my first book seems appropriate. This songbird, a phantom of my imagination, symbolized well my elusive dream of happiness, my otherworldly flights into youthful fantasy.

II.

I do not recall any time in my life when I was not involved with poetry. When I was a child just beginning to read, my favorite books, offered by my father from his well-stocked shelves, were Volume 17 of the Harvard Classics, Æsop's Fables, and a large, handsomely bound volume entitled, *Pearls from Many Seas*. This latter book contained a number of poems, and I always read those first before going on to some of the short prose pieces. The rhythm and diction of Tennyson's poem, "The Brook," held a particular fascination for me, and I kept returning to it.

It was in another book, *Negro Poets and Their Poems*, edited by Robert Kerlin and published in 1923, the year I was born, that I was first introduced to a handsome brown boy named Langston Hughes; I read with great enthusiasm his poem about being "Black as the night is black,/ Black like the depths of Africa." (Later, at the age of fourteen, I was to have the privilege of meeting him. Then in 1942, when I was a student at Virginia State College, he read some of my poems publicly during his reading there, subsequently including one of them in *The Poetry of the Negro, 1746-1949*, coedited with Arna Bontemps.) It was in Kerlin's book, also, that I first read poems by Paul Laurence Dunbar, James Weldon Johnson, Anne Spencer, and Georgia Douglas Johnson. I still treasure my father's bust of Dunbar, sculpted by Isaac Hathaway in 1915, now in my possession; it had been on display in my home for as long as I could remember.

I was about five when my father brought home a Philadelphia clergyman, already aged but tall and still erect, who had written the words and music to many of the hymns we sang in church. The Rev. Charles A. Tindley made a tremendous impression on me, and my continued appreciation of his hymns has been deepened by my having met him at a very impressionable age.

There was also my mother's old "elocution" textbook, which she had used as a normal school student at what is now Virginia State University. I spent countless hours reading poems from it aloud, committing some to memory.

How natural that, whenever I felt a deep emotional need, I turned toward creating poems of my own! The two-year residence of my cousin Helen with my family had helped to relieve the loneliness from which I had always suffered in a boy-dominated home and neighborhood. Her presence gave me the much-needed companionship I craved. When she and her mother moved to Richmond, I was devastated by the loss. It was then, at about the age of ten, that I wrote "The Reason Why I'm Lonely," pleading for someone to come and take her place.

As my father prepared for a summer in Europe, Africa, and the Holy Land in 1934, I feared greatly for his safety; the Atlantic Ocean seemed so incredibly vast and threatening! Writing a poem was the only way I could cope with my apprehension.

By the time I was twelve, I had counted one hundred original poems, many of which had been published in the mimeographed Ashland Grammar School newspaper. (After that, I stopped counting.)

On October 30, 1935, the youth section of the Orange (NJ) *Daily Courier* gave me my first real credit with the publication of "My Choice":

> At day I see the pretty flowers
> Touched by nature's hand,
> At night I see the twinkling stars
> All over Heaven Land.
>
> And if I had my choice of where
> I'd rather have my birth,
> I don't know whether I would choose
> To live on heaven or earth.

One of those first hundred poems, "Welfare Days," reflects my limited knowledge of the Depression, which I had heard discussed by my parents, as well as by visiting church members who sometimes came to the parsonage with their problems. I was also aware of strange men who occasionally came to the back door asking for food or money. But contrary to Professor Sedlack's assumption, my optimism during this period was not forced. We were indeed poor, but we didn't know it because all the other families with whom we had close contact were worse off than we were. Never mind that my mother dressed me in hand-me-down clothing, including my brother's outgrown coats, and subjected me to the embarrassment of long underwear tucked inside cotton rib stockings while my white classmates wore short socks under stylish snow suits. She could take a cupful of leftovers and make enough hash to feed an army; we were never hungry. No matter that my father voluntarily reduced his already low salary as a minister to twenty-five dollars a month. During the same period, he earned two additional academic degrees, attended the World Baptist Alliance in Berlin, and occasionally, on a fine spring Sunday morning, appeared in his pulpit resplendent in a morning coat. And every summer we spent a few days on the beach in Long Branch and visited my maternal relatives in Richmond. Dad had a job, and my mother, trained as a teacher, stayed home to raise her children in an atmosphere of love and security.

Around 1936 my father taught adult classes in sociology and Negro literature under the sponsorship of the Works Progress Administration of New Jersey. *An Anthology of Negro Poetry*, the mimeographed text for the literature course, compiled with the assistance of Langston Hughes, Countee Cullen, and Sterling Brown, gave me further opportunities for reading poetry by people with whom I could identify.

(Four years later, I would receive a letter of encouragement from Sterling Brown and in 1944 I would have the privilege of visiting Countee Cullen in his home where he told me, after reading some of my work, "Well, you're a poet!")

Also in 1936, my parents decided to feature me on a church program to recite poetry I had memorized, including some of my own. I was joined by an accomplished high school pianist who played several classical selections.

About the same time, my poetry became the vehicle for the romantic yearnings I had begun to feel for boys my brothers brought home from school and others I knew at church. I guarded these compositions as best I could, along with the first of many journals, from the prying eyes of family members.

In spite of the exposure I had to poetry by African Americans, it was the literature I studied at school which influenced my writing the most. The emphasis on Romantic and Victorian English poets, along with a few Americans such as Longfellow, locked me into unnatural patterns of diction, rhyme, and meter. (The classical curriculum which I selected at East Orange High School was continued at Sumner High School in St. Louis, with an emphasis on Latin, Shakespeare, Homer and Tennyson's *Idylls of the King.*)

My family's move to St. Louis, Missouri in December, 1937, and my enrollment at the all-black Sumner High School represented a dramatic turning point in my life. My emotional state in New Jersey had been tested by the turmoil of being the only child of color in all my classes through eighth grade. Subtle and overt evidences of racism were always present in the classroom, and I suffered from a deep sense of alienation and rejection. Still, I had managed to meet the challenge, regularly earning A's in English, seeing many of my poems printed in the school paper, and having the teacher show movies my father had taken in Egypt to my sixth grade ancient history class. But I was constantly reminded of the limitations placed on me by a school system which did not employ a single African American—in *any* capacity.

Now, in spite of the deepening anguish of adolescence, the encouragement of administrators, teachers, and fellow students at Sumner and the support of the community at large gave me the desire to excel and offered rewards which I could not have expected in the former setting. The 1938 yearbook included some of my poems along with an article written about me by one of my classmates. Other poems appeared with regularity in various Sumner High School publications. At fifteen I made my first appearance on the radio reading several of my poems, and various community groups invited me to participate in public programs, often along with my schoolmate, baritone Robert McFerrin. I entered and won several literary contests, one of which was judged by a cousin of Sara Teasdale, a poet in her own right. She took an interest in my work, visiting me in my home, and was responsible for submitting one of my poems to the *Missouri School Journal*, giving me my first national exposure. During my junior or senior year I was one of only three high school students in all of St. Louis to win recognition in the national art and literary contest sponsored annually by *Scholastic Magazine*.

It would be a few years yet, however, before I would escape completely from the archaic diction of European poetry of another era, as evidenced in the embarrassing poem of 1943, "To a Man with Wings," written for my brother when he became a fighter pilot with the now-famous Tuskegee Airmen.

III.

In preparing *Remembrances of Spring* for publication, I made no attempt to include all the early poems for which I still have copies. They are many. (Unpublished and uncollected poems are available at the Special

Collections Library at Fisk University.) It is only those which have been collected and are no longer easily accessible which I wished to make available. *Songs to a Phantom Nightingale* and *One and the Many* are presented in their entirety. Most of the poems in *Phantom Nightingale: Juvenilia* are also included; several written prior to high school or thought to be repetitive in style and content have been omitted. *One and The Many* is here, not only because it is out of print but more importantly because some of the poems were written during my college years before I reached the age of twenty-one.

Organization of the book posed a problem. I was tempted to place poems in their chronological order as nearly as possible, regardless of the collections in which they first appeared, but I concluded that it would be preferable to keep the integrity of the original volumes intact. The several poems which appeared in more than one collection are given in the order of their first publication. While *Juvenilia* was not published until 1981, the dates of composition place most of the poems earlier than those of *One and the Many*, making for an awkward arrangement, but no solution presented itself.

As an aid to the reader, I have frequently listed on the left, after the poem, the actual or approximate date of composition, as nearly as I can determine it. During certain periods I was meticulous in recording dates of completion; at other times, I made no note of them, having now to rely on memory. On the right appear the dates and/or places of original publication when I could verify them.

In spite of a strong temptation to edit many of these poems, I exercised considerable restraint, leaving them in their original state. To do otherwise would have destroyed the integrity of the work and rendered the collection useless.

Now at the age of seventy and far removed from the sweet trilling of my early nightingale, I hope that this collection will be useful, not only in documenting the development of an individual poet, but also as encouragement and a beacon light for other young persons who may be testing the literary waters now as I was doing then.

NLM
July 5, 1993

Songs to a Phantom Nightingale

2

Song to a Phantom Nightingale

Oh, nightingale that lures my soul to slumber,
That makes me happy when my world goes wrong,
That brings me notes of love in endless number
And makes my life a free and endless song;

Where will you be when nights are dark and dreary?
Where will you be when skies are never blue?
Will I still hear your songs when I am weary,
Or must I bid your love a sad adieu?

And will you sing when skies are grey and sorrow
Comes down in torrents like the falling rain?
You sing a song tonight, but on tomorrow
Must I be sad and lonely once again?

Ah, sighing winds that ripple like the river,
Oh, restless tree tops, vague as in a dream,
Dear phantom nightingale, you were not ever
The songster that to me you always seem.

A Sumner High School publication
1938

RACE

Tonight
Fate and I run swiftly—
Fate for her desire
And I for mine.
Both cannot win.

As we run on this track,
Panting,
Breathless,
Yet determined not to lose,
Who is watching us?
Who shall decide
If Fate shall win
Or I?

The Challenger
June 1940

VIA DOLOROSA

Help me to forget
That flowers die
And embers die
And old loves die.

I loved a rose
So fair and fragrant,
While it bloomed.
And then—
I wrote its epitaph.

There was a glow
Deep in my heart
That was my happiness.
Then came the snow
And rain.
My flame burned out.

Roses, embers, old loves—
All alike.
They go the way of sorrow
And kill my happiness
When they die.

THE STORM

The giant is furious tonight!
He paces back and forth across the floor
Which is heaven.
He stamps and rages
Until the clouds turn black with fright.
He speaks in angry, maddening tones;
Fire—white fire—rushes from
His frothing lips and lights the gloom.
The giant is battling with his soul—
His will.
Great drops of sweat fall from his brow;
Salty tears and agonized drops of sweat
Mingle, as they fall in sweeping torrents,
Driven downward by the giant's uneven breathing.
And through it all,
I sleep in unrestful peace;—
I, too, am battling with my will.
But in the morning when I 'wake,
A clear blue sky greets me.
The giant is friendly
And he sends a ball of gold across the horizon—
His apology . . . . .
That night, I can see
The giant's gorgeous array of diamonds
Spread out on a blue-covered table,
And the silver trophy that he won
In the battle with his soul.
Yes, he is a man of many moods.
Perhaps that is why his silver trophy
Is partly covered with fearful clouds
And a storm now threatens.

THERE WAS ONE NIGHT

There was one night when he who dug the pit
Escaped its torture; he who sought for gold
Found gold, and he who sowed the seed of strife
And mad confusion reaped a joy three-fold.

I saw old Pilate with his dripping hands
Washed clean of blood, and Tantalus bending low
His weary head contented with his fruit
Broke off the spell that cursed him long ago.

That night doomed cities rose to greet the moon
While fallen armies sang of victory;
Styx was a river of the living blood
Where lovers met in starlit ecstasy.

There was one night when I, too, roamed my fields
Free and unfettered and released at last
To soar along high places; free to leave
Old unrelenting phantoms of my past.

ca. 1938

MISCONCEPTION

I shall remember how we met and parted
Upon the hill at dusk of every day
To greet the first star in its shy appearance,
And bid farewell the flaming sun's last ray.

Oh when we met, Apollo in his glory
Cast all his radiant beauty on your hair,
And twilight's gleaming roseate hues were mingled
With morning stars that still were lingering there.

What witchery the purple shadow uses
On dark'ning hillsides in the setting sun!
I used to think your eyes were truly lighted
With precious gems and pure gold finely spun.

Now that I see you, not in flame and sunshine,
But by the frigid bleakness of the sea,
My sad heart whispers just how dull and tarnished
And stripped of gold you have turned out to be.

ca. 1939

8

In Springtime

The leaves are green, the world is new,
And life is sweet when skies are blue;
I love to sit and dream of you
In springtime.

My worldly fancies turn to dreams
Of starlit skies and rippling streams,
Of green hillsides and soft moonbeams
In springtime.

I cannot help but spend the night
Fashioning fantasies of light
Then joining them in silent flight
In springtime.

Some day I'll have a peaceful mind
Knowing that all my life I'll find
Sweet life, sweet love. Fate will be kind
Some springtime.

WHEN I WAS YOUNG

When I was young and loved life's laughter
I climbed tall hills and touched the sun;
I did not know till long years after
That ecstasy and pain are one.

But now that I have ceased pursuing,
My laughter has been hushed by Time
For pain is all left for renewing;
There are no more tall hills to climb.

The St. Louis Call or
The St. Louis Argus
ca. 1940

TO AUTUMN

I do not scorn your gay approach
And your bewildered laughter; still
You sadden me with your mild touch
When you appear over the hill.

Though frost glows in your dancing eyes
And though your leaves with scarlet burn,
I cannot say that I despise
Your gloomy smile or your return.

THE MOON BELOW ME

I am standing on a mountain-top
Gazing at the moon
Which is below me.

A milk white steed races by
Which I halt
And mount.
We run across the plains
And down the hills
Toward the moon,
Still below us.

An eagle soars through space,
And I catch it.
I climb upon its back
While it flies down, down,
In the direction of the moon.

I am wondering what the moon is
As the eagle, which bears me,
Soars downward through the night.
Perhaps it is composed of white hot fire
Which melts and burns
All souls in agony,
And mingles sin into a ball of torment
That we call hell.

If this is the moon,
I must command my white eagle
Which is flying downward with my soul
To turn and flee to the mountains
From whence it came;
Lest my sinless soul,
Borne by the eagle,
Melts in the moon
Which is below me.

SILENCE

I have learned to be silent.
My life's oppression,
Suppression
Have made me so.
One time my soul cried out
For expression
Of transgression:
One time it was hushed
And left bleeding,
Crying,
Dying.

So I have learned the world's lesson:
Silence,
Hushed longings,
Warped desires,
Smoldering fires,
Muffled hearts throbbing,
Sobbing
Soft in a pillow
In the dark.

I have learned to be silent.

ca. 1940

BECAUSE I CAN

I smile because I can smile—
Because I wear the crown of victory
Over despair;
Because there is sunshine in my life
That casts no shadows.

I know joy;
I am a friend to happiness;
Content and I walk hand in hand
Through sunlit meadows.
So I smile.

I laugh because I can laugh;
For I am fearless,
Dauntless,
Proud of my fulfilled desire.

I know blue skies
And youth and tenderness.
I know green fields
And intimacy with God.
So I can smile—
And I do.

The Challenger
June 1940

14

STYX BEFORE CROSSING

Come along, Charon, the night's growing older
Here on the bleak, barren sands of this shore;
And I can see that the river's much colder
Than it was two or three hours before.

Come along, come along, why do we linger?
Life's day is ended; the farce has been played;
Dead is my heart beat and numb is my finger,
Hushed is my yearning: I am not afraid.

Night covers all with its black starless cover;
Into its velvet the white moonbeams blend;
I am a princess and you are my lover,
Luring me on to my destiny's end.

Why should I care if my heart has been broken,
Dipped in its blood and anointed with rain?
All hope is lost for the dire fates have spoken:
Love and contentment will come not again.

Why do you stand there and stare as if dreaming?
Haven't you learned not to reckon with fate?
Bring out your raft while the moon is still gleaming.
Come along, Charon, the night's growing late.

THE AFTERGLOW

I can remember the deep shadows' gloom
'Mid happiness once long ago;
I still recall that dim, amber room,
But oh, the afterglow!

Sometimes I cry as I sit in the haze
Of the twilight; all sorrow I know
As I think and remember my happiest days.
And now the afterglow.

I live again all the scenes of the past,
Before my life's fire burned low.
That was joy; but I realize now, at last
This is the afterglow.

ca. 1937

16

WRITTEN ON THE LAST OF APRIL

So now it is your time to leave me,
To shake the rain from your hair,
To brush the tears from your dawn-gray eyes
And say goodbye.

Then say good-bye, my friend,
And leave me.
Why delay? Why linger still mutely
While your brief hour passes?

This is all, then, is it not?
Good-bye, my friend,
My dawn-eyed love;
Goodbye, April.

SING SOFT AND LOW

Sing soft and low; don't wake my thoughts
But let me go on dreaming
Lest I may realize that life
Is not the moonlight's gleaming.

Sing soft and low; let life be sweet
And naught but drunken madness
Lest joy may strangely disappear
And leave the world in sadness.

Paint all my shadows bright and gay
As sorrow goes a-winging
So that my heart will always love
The sweet song you are singing.

ca. 1937

SPRING IN SAINT LOUIS

I haven't heard a robin sing,
I haven't seen a bud appear,
Nor have I seen a sprig of grass
Peep through the frosty earth this year.
    I haven't seen
    The lake thaw out—
    Frog leap about—
    World turn to green;
No, all along the country-side
The world is still its dying brown,
And Winter still stalks cruelly
Along the streets of this old town.

But yesterday a smokeless sun
Fell on my window bright and clear,
And glist'ning through the smokeless air,
It made me know that spring is here.

ca. 1940

THE CITY

This is a shining city gay and bright,
In whose white glow souls lost in futile dreaming
Are hidden in the spangle of the night,
And young eyes soon forget their silent gleaming.

Upon the hope that grief may be forgot,
Our frail and wounded souls are ever feeding;
But though they grasp for glitter, gold or not,
Weep for the muffled hearts that still are bleeding.

Here where a thousand heart throbs sound as one,
Life is the nectar drop drained from a bottle;
We drink but once and when the toast is done,
The mighty Engineer turns off His throttle.

If ever you should pass along this way,
Remember that I wrote this little ditty;
And glancing from your window, smile and say:
"Green fields were not for her; she loved the city!"

The Challenger
June 1940

No Stars Tonight

No stars tonight, no moon,
No birds to sing;
Love's gone a-miss
And joy has ceased to be.
My garden flow'rs are dead.
Alas, their withered leaves
Look up and laugh at me!

No song in my heart,
No singing in my soul
Save this blue melody.
Clouds fill the sky
And gray mist is the air;
Look up and see.

No moon in sight;
Only a dead white rose
That someone tall and dark
Has loved.
Only an empty garden,
And no stars tonight
To see it by.

Love's over now.
I rest my weary head
To greet a sleepless dream
Without night's diamond gleam—
Without the stars.

ca. 1937

IF THIS BE A DREAM

If this be a dream, don't wake me.
If I should wake to find
This all a fantasy,
I could not bear the pain.

If this be a dream, let thunder-storms
And rolling seas awake me not
To find that life is empty
And stripped of all its pleasures.

If all this is unreal,
Show me the peaceful calm
Of rippling waters,
Let me bathe therein and never
Find myself again.
Let me die before I wake
If this be a dream.

DEPARTURE OF SUMMER

Summer is waving her hand sadly
And her whole being is melancholy;
But a spark of hope flashes in her eye
As she whispers: "I'll be back again."

Summer is going away.
She carries a brown satchel in her hand
And casts a wistful eye over her shoulder
As she departs.

She shakes the green leaves of her hair
And speaks in the mellow tone
Of her rippling streams.
I shall surely miss the warmth of her breath.
I am melancholy, too,
Knowing that Summer is leaving,
Although hope glitters in her eye;
Although she promises that she'll be back.

CANOSSA*

I've been to Canossa;
Known its death-cold snows
And misty winter skies.

I've been depressed;
Suffered pain that cut as deep
As the snow itself.

I've battled against cruel hearts,
Numb, frozen hearts as cold
As Canossa's winter.

I know just what it means
To find life's sweetest dreams
Cannot come true.

But I've hoped against
Canossa's blinding storms.
And lo, I am the victor!

A Sumner High School publication
1938

---

* A ruined castle in northern Italy where Henry IV, a German emperor of the Holy
Roman Empire, who had been excommunicated by Pope Gregory VII, did penance
in 1077 by standing barefoot in the snow.

24

FROM
Phantom Nightingale: Juvenilia

ACHIEVEMENT

The stars on high, flickering now,
Shine for a while but find their light
Too glamorous to twinkle on,
Too gloriously bright.

The leaves and flowers wake to find
Life not as sweet as first it seemed
So close their weary eyelids, sad
That they have ever dreamed.

Man, man alone must stand steadfast.
He must endure, forget, forgive
Since God first molded him of clay
And said, "Now breathe and live."

We drift along and race to join
The future of uncertainty
While new things come to take the place
Of those that cease to be.

More than the daylight in the sky
The world needs men—men to endure
While ceaseless ages come and go—
Strong men, dauntless, secure.

Young men and women, stand up strong.
The toughest blows in life receive
With not a faltering heart or hand:
Here lies the power to achieve.

ca. 1938   A Sumner High School publication

27

AUTUMN NIGHT

The leaves are turning brown again
And frost is in the air.
I'm walking through the town again
In sorrow and despair.

I see a speeding train tonight.
I hear the lark's last call.
I think there may be rain tonight
For now I face the fall.

There is no crescent moon for me
As I go through this town.
Joy faded all too soon for me—
The leaves are turning brown.

ca. 1940   *The Virginia Statesman*
                December 6, 1941

AUTUMNAL

Oh, take my hand for one more time
And then, goodbye.
The birds must make their southward flight
And so must I.

I must have known those nights I lay
And watched you smile
This moon was never meant to shine
But a brief while

Until, like ash of burned-out flame
Once gay and bright,
It too must turn to dust and sigh
Its last goodnight.

But ever in this bleeding heart
There will remain
A wistful medley of dead leaves
And autumn rain.

ca. 1941

MEMORIAL

They have fled like the green of the heath and the hill;
Like the birds going south have they flown,
And of all the bright dreams I have cherished and loved
None is left to be kept as my own.

I have wept, I have wailed like the winds of the deep,
But like leaves turning brown in the fall,
They have withered and died, they have scattered and blown
From my life past the reach of my call.

I am silent tonight, for a dream that is dead
Is a ghost of the dust-laden years,
And like trees being stripped of their leaves by the wind,
O my Soul, I am stripped of my tears.

ca. 1941

Ann G. Kurdt, ed., *America Speaks*
(New York: Horizon House, 1942)

On Parting

Trudge over the hill, Autumn,
Trudge over the hill with your arm about him.
Take him away if you must
But when you come back to me,
Make sure that he is with you.

ca. 1940

LAMENT

This is September: see the red leaves flying, flying.
If I were Love, perhaps I might fly, too,
And never feel regret for your branches
Bared to cruel winds.

Were I the sun, I might shine brightly, brightly
To glare and blind your eyes like Truth,
Or if in rain I might fall on the pavement
Of your heart,
Perhaps like Fear I might crush you to the ground.

This is September, but
I am not leaf or rain or sun—
And you are all.

ca. 1940

32

In Pursuit

Today I walked a thousand miles
And missed not one;
I climbed a thousand hills in search
Of one bright sun.

But every mile was covered with
Dead leaves and brown,
And from each hill that I climbed up
I fell back down.

Still though the darkness comes to blight
The half-dark gloam,
The longest mile, the steepest hill
Is my way home.

ca. 1940

FROM THE SHELTER

Brown leaf catching too much sun,
Gray street, too much rain.
Who can tell a lonely heart
Spring will come again?

Who can lead a hungry sheep
To a dying fold
When the soul is stripped of love
And the heart is cold?

You may pledge the windy plain,
For the summer's gone,
But while lingers still the night,
Promise not the dawn.

I, who staggered forth from dusk
Into deeper night
Dare not bruise my heart again
In pursuit of light.

ca. 1940

IN ABSENCE

I miss you this time every year
The way I miss the spring
When I pretend that I can hear
The songbirds echoing.

I feel your absence as I feel
The winter's biting chill;
I miss you when the white snow falls
Upon the quiet hill.

When I remember how I loved
The ocean's rise and fall,
This is the time I want you near
And miss you most of all.

ca. 1940

TO MARCH

Farewell, March, I shall not miss you
When you go—
Your changing hours of sun and rain,
Of wind and snow.

I never knew a more inconstant
Friend than you
For you are like a trusted lad
Who proved untrue.

I hear you, faithless braggart, laughing
At my pain,
Amused that I should look for strength
In April's rain,

But go on laughing; your brief hour ends
With the dawn.
Farewell, March. I shall not miss you
When you've gone.

March 31, 1940

ADVENT

I am shuddering in my heart, for soon it will be spring and
    spring does not mean lilacs any more.
I have thought of tables set for two on shadowed terraces,
    and chinks of morning sun across closed lids.
I have remembered robins' throats pulsing with song and the
    wings of eagles stretched across the infinite azure of my
    skies.
Elysian meadows have I known to yield their fruits of
    promise to receptive hearts;
But I have seen my meadows wither and their fruits, chill-
    blasted, fall upon the ground.
I have tried to forget that my robins have flown south and
    my eagles gone to roost,
But I cannot obliterate my terraces now lost in brumal
    slumber beneath the copper disc that was the sun.
I am quaking in my heart, for May has come to mean the
    drone of prolonged rain, and the quivering river will
    never again break through to greet the spring,

Maroon and White,
June 1941

SUNDAY AFTERNOON

Sunday clothes and parlor pipes,
Lily-scented hair,
Red plush Bible on the shelf,
Cuckoo on the stair,

Shining patent leather shoes
Garbing tiny feet
For a slow walk through the town
On a quiet street,

Blossoms on the thawing lake:
Dear familiar things
Fragrant of the thousand hopes
Of a thousand springs.

Sip the drunk perfume of May
With a sigh, and then,
Past the rows of green front lawns,
Parlor pipes again.

Maroon and White
June 1941

In Search of You

My tired eyes unceasingly
Have searched the wide world through and through
Just hoping in their wandering
To catch a glimpse of you.

My ears have listened though at times
Hope seemed to take her way a-wing,
Listened to hear an echo of
The songs you sing.

Night and day through joys and tears
My heart like rhythmic drums has beat
For that one chance to make my life
A joy complete.

Something foretold a certain bliss,
And so I searched for brighter skies
To still the beating of my heart
And soothe my weary eyes.

Now I have found you; God forbid
that "through the years" these skies of blue
Will ever darken and make vain
My search for you.

January 18, 1938

REJECTION

I heard you sing to someone
And wondered how I'd feel
If you should sing to me.

Then my dreams came true
And I had all in life I desired,
But not for long.
Something happened and
You cast me to the winds.

Now someone else's smile inspires you
When you lift your voice.
I turn my head and pretend never to care,
But . . . .
I hear you sing to someone else
And recall the thrill I felt
When first you sang to me.

March 25, 1938

INVITATION

Drink in the night with me, the blue, cold night;
Walk with me toward the rising moon
Till time grows old.
Retard the tempo of my footsteps.
I know of a silence that falls like music
To the beat of feet on sidewalks.

I am grateful to the boy who whistles a tune I used to love.
I am thankful for the woman who laughs from the window
And for the traffic's din in which I lose myself.
Long years and disillusioned youth;
For loneliness, those blinking, distant river lights.
Come walk with me and I will show you.

We, we: two planks of driftwood drifting,
Touching, yet fated in the end to drift apart.
Drink in the night with me—time flies . . . . .
I know of a silence that can ease all hurt.

ca. 1940

41

WHAT PETER SAID

I have seen a new world
From a new hill
Steep as my hopes are
And deep as my heart.

Little caged bird
That nestles close in my soul,
Here from this hilltop
Fly as you were meant to fly;
I shall heal your wounded wing.

There is a star that shines
More brightly
Than I have ever seen it.
Go, go, little sparrow
Nourished by my blood.
Your freedom has been purchased
This day on the hill.

And all who come and go
In the hereafter
Will pause a while
And see my star
And hope again.

ca. 1939   *The Challenger*

HERITAGE

Look out, look out on yonder world,
That slender steeple,
That monument to Pluto filled
With laughing people.

Look out upon tall gods engaged
In merry-making;
The world fenced in can all be yours
Just for the taking.

I give to you a dance, a song
Borne by winged swallows,
And then I give you sleep to soothe
The pain that follows.

Take all the world I offer you
And laugh your laughter,
For there is only loneliness
In the hereafter.

July 28, 1940

HIGH NOON

Let us run and clap our hands;
Laughter is sweet.
This is the high noon of our heyday.
Let us traverse these sweeping,
Swinging slopes
This noonday
In the sunlight.
I am a pagan in my heart.
How I worship the image of the sun
In which your face is!
I am a heathen
And I cannot see those hills
For watching you.
Let us laugh and run
In the wind
Before night falls,
For love is forgotten easily
As fires burn out in rain.

The Challenger   December 18, 1940

PURCHASE

I like the smell of new clothes,
The novel aroma of challenge.
This dress has no past
Linked with regretful memories
To taint it,
Only a future as hopeful
As my own.
I can say of an old garment
Laid away in a trunk:
"This lace I wore on that day when . . . . "
But I prefer the new scent
Of a garment unworn,
Untainted like the new self
That I become
When I first wear it.

ca. 1940

DREAM BOATS

Oh, we must set our little boats adrift
Upon a ripple of our shallow streams
And hope a balmy breeze will fill their sails
And guide them to the ocean of our dreams.

Some boats may venture to a southern isle;
A few may seek the charm of old Cathay,
Some wander to the Land of Midnight Sun.
Many will not leave the tranquil bay.

But to the Sovereign who keeps our skiffs
We all must pray, however small they be,
That someday, anchoring on that distant shore,
We may announce that we have seen the sea.

February 1, 1940

DIRGE

If this must be the destiny
to which I have come,
pour the wine faster
and into a deeper cup.
Let the fear which now envelops me
drown in the lethal tide,
then, fire, consume.
Spartan-like, I shall not either wince
nor feel the pain.

Drink to the flame which, I fear,
will not leave my naked soul unsinged.
Ah, toast the twilit deluge
and the leaden dawn
which I must know.
Spare not the wine that cures all hurt.

If this must be my fateful denouement,
pour, pour the wine
into the vessel
of my twisted soul.
And so to Hell!

Maroon and White
June 1941

47

LAMENT TO TANTALUS

How could I know how long the night would be?
That in spilled wine would lie the destiny

Of noons, of midnights, and the tolling bell
From twelve to twelve? Great drops of water fell

So easily! How could I ever guess
That day could hold such barren hopelessness?

      Dawn breaks;
      Fate takes
         Her spoils.
      Day ends.
      Branch bends,
         Recoils

In endless cycles. Drunk with thirst and pain,
I weep. Oh Lachesis, where is the rain?

The Challenger
December 18, 1940

OUR CUPS ARE FULL

We said, If it should rain, why should we care?
We are not prophets. Anyhow
See how whitely beams the moon.
What if our cups run dry?
What if our stars should fall?
Ah, but they have not fallen, we said;
This is today.

In the east our star shines on.
Hesperus of the evening? Perhaps.
I think it has grown bright.
Our cups are yet full
And it is not raining.

But I am afraid what we shall find
Before the end.
How much more wine shall we need
When this is gone?
How many stars?
What moons?

The Challenger
December 18, 1940

ON DEMOCRACY

I heard the bugles blowing
And I saw the flag unfurled;
I heard them call this country
The fairest in the world.

I heard their voices singing
For America the Free,
And I heard their praises ringing
For this land's democracy.

But for their fair land and country
I hadn't the slightest hope,
For my heart was with a Georgia man
Suspended from a rope.

I seemed to hear their laughter
Filled with hate and jeers
As he dangled in the moonlight.
I could see the bitter tears

Of a mother down in Georgia—
Saw her black face torn with fright
For the son whose body glistened
In the cold October night.

Blow your bugles! Sing your praises
For your white democracy!
But you've lynched a man in Georgia
And left him on a tree.

Maroon and White
June 1939

CROSS

Tonight
I left a white cross
On a grave.

Tonight
I left a wreath of white roses
Freshly picked
In the forest.

A prayer I prayed,
A song I sang
In the midst of sorrow,

For my heart, it is dead,
It is buried,
It is forgotten.
See, I left but a white cross for it,
So little I care.

April 27, 1940

TOO LATE

He kept imploring me to wait
And I kept saying No,
So now my feet are veins of steel
Implanted in the snow.

He kept reminding me that hearts
Could be as cold as stone
That palpitated ice, not blood:
I should not go alone.

But I, I was too blind to read
The message in the skies
Which swore that he who once fell prey
To dreams would never rise.

I could not hear the echoing
Of his heart-heavy pleas
Which fell upon the gray stone casts
Of other Niobes.

In vain he begged me not to leave
Until he too could go
And stand with me on feet of steel
Hard frozen in the snow.

And now my helpless tears drip down
On lips that have grown dumb,
And deafened ears await the beat
Of steps that will not come.

Maroon and White
June 1941

ESCAPE #2

My last night of bondage:
Your last night in town.
Oh, see how the raindrops
In torrents come down!

The wind whistles fiercely
And bends every tree;
It sings of oppression
And dark agony.

But I am not downcast
Though thunder may roll,
For dawn will bring freedom
And light to my soul.

You're leaving tomorrow:
The shackles I wear
Linked with your smile
And your lips and your hair,

The chains that enslave me,
The bars that I face
Will weaken and soon
They will slide out of place.

And I'll smile triumphantly
When you depart
Knowing that I hold
The key to my heart.

Oh, let the rain fall
In its gray agony,
But I shall not grieve
When you set my heart free.

October 22, 1939

Somewhere in London

The rain's falling somewhere in London;
The gray torrents sing of despair.
A dark cloud hangs over the city
In sorrow because you are there.

I woke from a sweet dream this morning
And greeted a bright golden dawn.
My life will be sunny and cloudless
And joyful—because you are gone.

1939

Plea for My heart's Sake

I know you think of me when you are lonely
And only dubious clouds command your sky.
I know that in the silent hush of evening
When shadows fall it is for me you sigh.

I never doubt that, where the rushes thicken
In some lost, God-forsaken wilderness,
A quaint remembrance makes your pulses quicken
And it is my remembrance that you bless.

But in the city's turbulent obsession,
Blind in the glaring lights, deaf in the scream
Of jazz refrains and dancers gaily swaying,
Will you forget me and the white moon's gleam?

When you come back to lights and wine and music,
I beg you not to need me any less,
For if you love me in your silent sorrow,
Then love me also in your happiness.

ca. 1941

SUPPOSITION

If I could have spoken,
I would have told you how the days
   drag slowly,
   slowly
   without end.
If I could have made words come,
I would have fallen
   at your feet,
   crying your name
   to yonder mountain-top.
I would have said:
   "Look at the sun,
   the rain,
   the dew;
   If you go, they go, too."

But I stood there
   mutely watching you go,
   knowing that you were deaf,
   that you could not comprehend
   the meaning of words
   and bended knees.
Silent like the phantoms of the morning
You hurried through the mist.
Blind and deaf and determined you were.

Why, then, should I try to hold you with mere words
When stone walls could not have held you,
When iron balls and chains
   could not have kept you here?

Better that I kept silent when you left,
Silent and proud as you were.

ca. 1939

MARTHA

Ah, such a child she was,
So young to be so old!
Not more than two years back
We talked, two adolescent girls,
And laughed about the things of life
We couldn't understand.
Then suddenly she changed,
And I saw her walk through lilies
To Lohengrin.
Then there was Johnny
And I watched her feed him.
So strange to hear a tiny voice
Calling little Martha "mommy"!

Two years
And she has gone through life—
Heaven, hell, and now—
Now death.

Martha lying silent as if asleep,
Johnny crying for milk
And no one to feed him.
Oh Martha, Martha,
So young to be so old!

ca. 1940

INCESSANT

And still the days went by. It seemed unjust
    That vultures should yet flap their cruel wings
While crosses mocked and shrieked, "In God we trust."

It seemed unreal that dear rose-scented things
    Should always after call to memory
The "glory" of which blinded nations sing.

Why did men shield their eyes? Would they not see
    The crimson hills of stained and reeking snow?
Could they not taste the gall that yet must be?

They said it soon must end; they wanted so
    To see the last soul lowered into dust,
But still the days went by—and still they go.

ca. 1941

THRENODY

Rain, rain upon my window;
Slow, slow the steps of feet
That walk in tom-tom rhythm
On my forsaken street.

The wind in blind confusion
Sobs out a sorrow song
Whose ebbing, throbbing echoes
My heart has known too long.

For Hope, the light of ages
In which I put my trust,
In pitiful surrender
Lies conquered under dust.

April 21, 1940   *The Challenger*
                    June 1940

59

AWAKENING

Hand in hand, we were going to conquer the world and save
    our souls—remember?
Idealistic trash, wasn't it?
We sit back complacently now and laugh about it over mugs of beer.
We were such innocent young fools then!
We are seasoned and sophisticated now
And what light of youth is still left in our eyes
    we shade in the blue dimness of a tavern,
    we disguise in the tragedy of laughter,
    we kill in the dawning after-hours.

Side by side, we were going to kneel in prayer to a God
And we would not lose.
Strange after all these years, isn't it, that once we thought the
    sun and wind and rain were God.
Let the band play a wild, wild song, for life is but a wild
    night and the morning after
And death is but an ash: tomorrow . . . .
Remember when we believed that after death came life again?

Ha! In this checker game, one cannot win.
Can you recall those foolish hours we wasted planning,
    scheming—for naught?
Last night Mac was thrown in jail for stealing bread.
How do we know what's right or wrong? Truth is unstable.
Mac's babies are starving, dying; so is the world.
Remember when, like thieves, we sought bread to feed the world?

Life's a mad game; better not to play it.
Better to give in and drift with the current.
We aren't children anymore—are we?

1941   Quill and Scroll Literary Supplement
                                       The Virginia Statesman
                                       May 2, 1942

SONNET

Rain, how I love thy dull, accented beat!
Yet how I loathe thy siren witchery
When, rushing, rushing forth to greet the sea,
Thy gray drops fall upon the lamplit street
And lure these two inconstant gypsy feet
Into an autumn night more cold than thee.
Irresolute, I follow thoughtlessly
To see thy flood the pathless ocean meet.
Then cold and wet, I turn my footsteps home
Past granite monuments that stand unmoved
By raindrops flowing down to boundless seas.
They feel no passionate impulse to roam.
They know no hunger who have never loved.
Oh, would that I were made of stone like these!

Maroon and White
June, 1941

To Bill

I drew a line between the past and present
That moment when I turned my back
And called, "I'll see you, pal."
That instant you became a memory
Belonging to my past. The present was
A long, slow walk away from you.

ca. 1939

FUNEREAL

I have dug you a grave
And laid you away in a cedar box
Amid a mountain of tissue paper
And blue ribbons
And the delicate scents of age-old dreams.
I have buried all that I could
But there is still left
A quick, sharp pain
Like a grain of salt in a wound.

ca. 1941   *The Virginia Statesman*
                  December 6, 1942

PIANISSIMO

Close the door when you go.
Shut out all the light.
Soon I shall draw the curtains.
When night comes
And I know you are far away,
I shall want no song nor laughter
Nor the music of children's feet
On the pavement.
I shall be far beyond the world.
Pianissimo . . . . . softly . . . . .
Very softly.
When you go, walk on velvet feet.
I shall not want the echo of your steps
To penetrate the carpeted halls
Of my silent palace.
Pianissimo . . . . .
Close the door when you go.
If you should ever knock again
You may not enter,
But come like mist at dawn
For I shall be sleeping
In a dreamless gloom.
Pianissimo . . . . .
Do not disturb me.

The Challenger
December 18, 1940

WITHOUT NAME

So near is my desire,
So certain is my goal,
So vivid is the fire
That burns within my soul,

So young am I in years,
So fresh and live and free
That grief and futile tears
Should be unknown to me.

I should not know dark skies
Or feel the kind of rain
That flows from troubled eyes;
Youth should be spared that pain.

Yet youthful ecstasy
And winter's bitter cold
Are mingled here in me—
I am both young and old.

ca. 1940

TO MY MOTHER

The wrinkles of your brow and the silver of your hair
Are plain to see.
They represent the crosses and the heavy weight of care
You bear for me.

When winter brings its snow and when summer shows its
                    flowers
I find you true.
I owe the life I live and a life of unlived hours,
Mother, to you.

I love the silver strands of the hair upon your head,
The untold bliss
Of endless happy nights when you tucked me into bed
And left a kiss.

Had I all I desire and a thousand lives to live
In hopefulness,
To you I'd owe these lives, and the gain I'd glad give
In thankfulness.

St. Louis Call
May 6, 1938

TEARS

Thank God for tears when cold hearts turn to stone,
The tears that free the soul from dark distress.
When sympathy is dead, and all alone
One spends a dismal night of hopelessness,
When one may neither dance nor sing nor die,
Thank God, he still may cry.

Be grateful for the walks down lamplit lanes
When mind and heart are patterned in despair.
Thank God for smoke and mist and falling rains
When comrades go their way and cease to care.
When hours of loneliness stretch into years,
Thank Him for blessed tears.

ca. 1940   *The Virginia Statesman*
                                  February 14, 1942

MARKET STREET

Dusky Harlem
Here in the Middle West—
Under the smoky street lamps
I hear your laughter
And know I have not escaped you yet.

I have known the Hudson too
On a starry night,
I have stood and watched too
The reflection of the Jersey lights
Across the water,
And I have gone back to my flat
In the west a hundred twenties
To the jazz and laughter,
To the footsteps on the sidewalks
Of my Harlem.

But never mind now.
This is my home, I say,
And the Mississippi calls me
Just the same.
I wander back to my flat
And the jazz, the laughter,
The footsteps are still in my ears,
And I know I have not gotten
Dusky Harlem out of my blood.

Across the miles,
Across the years,
The lights have not flickered.
Lenox Avenue, Harlem—
Market Street, St. Louis.
What difference does it make?
I turn away and shut my eyes,
For this throbbing, stamping,
Screaming red-hot rhythm
Follows my people wherever they go,
And I have not escaped it yet.

ca. 1940   *Maroon and White*, June 1941

68

ON A NARROW STREET

Here in this beamless alley,
Gray with rain,
Hazed with the chain of dreams
Youth links together endlessly,
Pause for a while—
A dim, brief, starless while—
And see this passage with a vision.

I think it beautiful
(You doubt me?)
In its cheerless gloom:
Tall tele-posts towering above us,
Light drizzle on the pavement,
And the silhouettes of ebon structures
Leaning against a steel-gray sky . . . . .
Proud youth, these are our heritage,
But one thing more: a flickering light.
Cling to it with your eyes,
Your soul,
Your being.

Our lives are alleys,
Beamless, gray with rain,
But not so bleak that here and there
A dim light does not shine.
Our task, to find it.

ca. 1940   *Maroon and White*
                            June 1941

TO A DREAM CITY, IN DEPARTING

I have given you what I could not give my dearest love.
How often have I walked your gray, smoke-shrouded streets
    to tell your darkness of my profoundest dreams.
How often have I confided in the shadows of your tall, dark
    buildings when my thoughts could find no other ear.
And the mornings (How many!) I have walked along your
    boulevards and seen the sun shine through—
Always the morning sun.

I have taken from the screech of your traffic, from the heart-
    cries of your disconsolate, busy, hurrying children, a
    peace and a purpose that no books can impart.
No years could have given me life at its fullest as you gave it.
You were my repose, my comfort, my mother.

How can I lose you, my city, after these years? Your broad
    streets are my veins; your fog, my soul.
When in my loneliness I long for you, how can I be content
    with other sidewalks, other brown leaves, other rain?

I shall come back to you if only in vision.
I shall yet build my dream house in your soil.
I shall remember . . . . . I shall remember . . . . .
You will still be my dawn.

1941

VIRGINIA

Through my veins pulses the sweet perfume of magnolia
And the poignant fragrance of pine.
In my blood throbs an age-old ecstasy
Of breezes blowing in from the ocean
And the white-winged pattern of gulls
Against the sky.

(Last night on the deserted street,
An old ghost whispered something about blossoms and laughter
And singing underneath the stars.
I think I know now why the soil is still damp
With the blood of warriors.)

Piercing the heavens with its swift, breath-taking sting,
Penetrating the earth with its slow, seeping sweetness,
The perpetual love of April:
Older than Richmond—
Younger even, than the heart of me!

ca. 1942

72

MIDNIGHT MAGNOLIAS

Who are you, black girl, that you should walk
Through these Virginia pathways free—
Smelling the flowers grown for white nostrils,
Leaving your prints where only white feet should tread?
Breathing free southern air?

These paths are dark now; the hour is late.
See here where in the heat of today
Young bridled horses ambled along—
Pedigreed horses, you call them;
Horses with an ancestral tree.

And what have I?
A run-down slave cabin in the Virginia back-hills;
A shawl my grandfather wore following John Brown;
A song that I sing and sing for fear
The tears may fall if I ever stop.

Listen:
I'm not your pedigreed horse
Or the St. Bernard you feed steak to while I go hungry—
I'm not even the kitten your drawling, yellow-haired
            children
Give thick, rich cream to lap.
I'm a Virginia colored girl with a medley of train wheels
Running through my brain
And names of places like Memphis and Chicago and Kansas
            City
And a yen for walking alone
And an ache for beauty—for green trees and magnolia
            blossoms.

I walk here while your highborn ladies,
Your blond children who learn "nigger" with their alphabet,
Your pedigreed horses, your dogs, your cream-fed kittens
Are asleep.

I walk here because I have nowhere else to be.
I press my lips to magnolia petals
Because I am weary and magnolias may be the last scent I
    ever know
And the softest kiss I'll ever feel again.

I hate your streets because your red-necked men of the
    corners
Say things when I pass, and when I turn my head away
They spit at me and call me "nigger."
I hate your kitchens for, although I use my hands to knead
    your bread
And nurse your newborn babies from my breast,
I must drink from a special glass marked "colored"
Because you say my lips are unclean.
I hate your colonial houses with their clean white columns
Because I was born in a dirt-floor shack
With a fly-swatter in my mouth
Instead of a silver spoon.
The only things I like in your "democratic," race-conscious
    south
Are the magnolias that you have not touched;
They still smell clean and sweet like God
And they do not close their scent to broad black nostrils.

Let me walk through God's garden in peace tonight.
Let me leave the print of black lips
On at least one thing in your world
Besides a "colored" drinking glass
Before I catch my train for Memphis or Chicago or Kansas
    City—
It doesn't matter which.

    Hey, gal! Get a move on ya!
    Them's white folks' flowers.

They don't grow black magnolias, you know—
Even in Virginia.

1942   *The Virginia Statesman*
                                       November 1942

SONG FOR A NEGRO

Sing me a song for a Negro.
Tell me wherein he is different.
Show me why he must bow beneath a separate load
And pray in an alien Gethsemane
For his cup to pass.

Sing me a song for a Negro
Telling me why he must suffer for being black;
Telling me where in the Book a dark man's destiny
Is said to be futile and forlorn;
Answering me why even a little child must pay.

Sing me a song for a Negro
Saying what desires and dreams he lacks
That white men know—
What scourges a black man can bear
That his brother can not.

Sing me a song for a Negro:
An ancient, weary hymn to a Jim-Crow God—
A jazz tempo that white feet will not dance to—
A love song with a mulatto moon in a tainted sky—
A lullaby expressly made for dusky infancy.

Find me a dream that black men do not dream;
A passion that black men do not feel.
Find me a song that black men do not sing.
Sing me a song for a Negro.

ca. 1942   *The Virginia Statesman*

JEREMIAD

We drink the bitter cup—we do not wail.
Though all about us flay and scourge
And the gall leaves bad tastes in our mouths,
We are a strong people
And we do not bow.

We do not beg for it to pass—
We only wait.
And in our hearts we sing a song
Born of the Deep South
And slave cabins
And slow, lazy rivers in July.
Of cotton fields and weary backs
Bending in the scorch of noon
We lift our voices.
We are a new Negro
But we sing an old song.

We bleed, we burn, we die,
And yet we smile and drink the cup
And grow stronger.

ca. 1940

TO A BROWN BOY

I love you for the puzzled way you smile
As if the sad and aged of our race
Had shed their tears upon you, and the young
Had carved their hope and courage in your face.

I love the ageless and unconquered steel
Of which your dreams are built. You seem to be,
From dark defeat to new, triumphant years,
A bridge whose span includes eternity.

ca. 1941

NEW HOUSE

There is nothing familiar about this house.
The rooms are new; the stairways have no dearly-known
    creak,
And even the piano sounds with a strange remote beauty.
There is no memory of you here
Crowding between these walls,
Rising like incense from the carpets,
Staring from every nook and cove,
Crying out from the alarm clock,
Being stirred in the morning cup.
I shall call my new home by the name of Hope:
I will forget you here!

I smile when I build such illusions in my mind
For other new houses have shown me their fallacy.
Other lands have been bright and fresh
And unbroken by the spade of remembering
Until all of a sudden, some trinket cried amidst the newness
That you were there.

There is nothing familiar about this house,
But though the rooms are new, the staircase sound
And the piano newly tuned,
You are a part of it—
I carry your memory in my heart;
I carry you across the threshold when I go.

1942

FROM A TENEMENT WINDOW

Foolish, incessant, inconsequential
Chatter . . .
Will it rain tonight?
The price of last week's sugar . . .
The style of hats,
Of tweeds . . .
The taste of canned
Tomato juice
And sirloin steak . . .
The baby's diet—
Damn!
Of all mean things to talk about . . .
To think about . . .
To dream about!
Can't you see? Are you blind?
Woman, the world's alive tonight.
Haven't you heard?
This night's a poem.
Listen to the fog horns
Out on the Sound,
The low, guttural moan
Of ignorance crying aloud
In a wilderness of tears.
Look at the harbor lights
Glistening and gleaming
Over the water. Smell the stabbing odor
Of a lost, wild sea.
Oh, the savor of salt!
Woman, listen.
Listen to the stars shattering
The fog.
Be silent, woman,
And listen to the world.

1942   *The Virginia Statesman*

MAY LAMENT

Why do the tears start?
How should I know?
Why do the doves coo,
Mournful and low?
　　Why is the sky gray?
　　Why does the dark day
Scream at me so?

Why is the May day
So unlike spring?
Why do the robins
Dolefully sing?
　　Where on this sad earth
　　Can there be found mirth
Gaily on wing?

Spring is for laughter—
I should be gay.
There should be happy
Singing for May.
　　There should be gladness—
　　Why, then, the sadness?
How can I say?

ca. 1943

PYRAMUS AND THISBE

They do not know, as they strive to keep us apart . . . . . Time wreaks
frailties even in the strongest barrier . . . . . the hardest stone . . . . .

In Babylon when Semiramis reigned,
There lived two lovers in whose hearts had sprung
A fire that parental love restrained;
Yet youth will loose its chains—and they were young.
So did they find, in that great wall of stone
Which kept them, although near, yet far apart,
A slender crack; and when they were alone,
If but in words, each gained the other's heart.
"Ah, Sweet, I hunger for the sight of thee;
The nights are drear and empty," he would say.
And in reply: "Down by the restless sea
When dew is fresh and faded is the day . . . . "

Meet me at the tomb of Ninus . . . Meet me at the white mulberry tree
. . . . .

"Wait by the cool, green spring; wait at the tree—
The old mulberry tree whose fruits are white.
And if thou waitest patiently for me,
Our surging hearts will find their peace tonight."
Forth did she go to keep her rendezvous,
A sheer and silken veil upon her head,
But ere the time her lover reached there, too,
In fear of death, she dropped her veil and fled.
For having caught his prey and missed the sword,
A vicious lion from the forest burst,
His lean jaws gory with their late reward,
And sought the fount to slake his eager thirst.
Upon the ground the veil in moonlight lay.
The lion thought to take it to his lair,
But after tearing it in bloody play,
He stalked away and left it lying there.

Prints of a lion . . . . . The veil . . . . . Thisbe's veil . . . . . Oh, hideous .
. . . . I die and these berries by my blood shall lose their blanched
purity . . . .

As Pyramus approached the wonted place,
He cast a downward look that snatched his breath;
A dread perception flashed across his face:
There lay the signs of Thisbe's tragic death—
A lion's footprints and the well-rent veil
All covered with the reeking scarlet stain!
Before his dreadful gaze the moon turned pale,
For he had come too late and all in vain.
"And I, who loved so well, by being late,
Have caused the death of Thisbe, fair and sweet.
I cannot live alone; oh, cruel fate,
By this my sword, Love's death shall be complete.
I, too, shall go and join her as she sleeps
And guard her as I failed to guard her life;
I, too, shall share the peace that follows strife."
So saying, Pyramus, with nerve like steel,
Pierced through his heart the weapon, blue, untried,
And smiled at death as though he did not feel
The young, courageous blood gush from his side.

Oh, Pyramus . . . . . Were we doomed to go on forever barely missing
each other . . . . . even in death . . . . .

When Thisbe ventured from the hollow stone
Which offered refuge from the forest-king,
At once she saw her lover lying lone
And bloody in the throes of suffering.
She called his name and clasped him to her breast;
He answered with a sigh as thin as air.
"Why was it, merciless and wicked beast,
That you forgot to drag me to your lair?
Far happier would I have been to know
That Pyramus, for reasons not in vain,
Had dyed these berries (once as white as snow)
To scarlet, with the essence of his pain.
The veil. The veil. For me my lover died;

For me he laid him down beside the sea.
Ah, I must stay forever by his side
And share his slumber—for he died for me!"

Strange fruit . . . . . *memorials of brave young blood* . . . . *defiant love*
. . . . . *two hearts at last made one* . . . . .

Who dares defy the right of youth to love
When Fate has smiled and given her consent?
When all the gods who rule the realms above
Are on one mission, one desire bent?
Who cannot give the whole gives not in parts;
Who may not be a lover is not friend.
He who would disunite two raptured hearts
Must weave for any tale a tragic end.
Old Circumstance, who builds a granite wall
To bar content and paint the future black,
Is due to witness her own hapless fall
When love detects some frailty or crack.
Give love its sway; bid friends and family
Bow down before its beauty and its truth.
Impulsive and short-lived as it may be,
Love is the essence and the pulse of youth.

That which sets out to gain soon loses much,
While losers gain (as in old Babylon).
Arousing ancient lovers with its touch,
The pulse of love instinctively throbs on.

ca. 1942

PASSING THE SIRENS

Nay, Captain, get you back into your bonds;
No witch's music shall enchant your soul
To sure destruction while we have our wits.
We will hold fast your wild, bewitchéd heart;
Our ears are filled until the peril's past.
I know a sweeter tune—Have you forgotten?—
Than siren's sorcery, a truer look
Than one that holds no lure of evening fires
And sons that wish their unseen fathers home.
Aye, purer music falls upon our minds
Though songs of sorcery would blot them out
For one brief moment while we pass the shore
Bound to our masts so that our carnal selves
May not deceive our soul selves. Ulysses,
Nine years have we prevailed against the gods,
Fierce, evil winds, and warring men. Shall we
Turn back now that our course is nearly done,
Having come thus far, fought so much wrong and won?
Get back into your bonds; no longer strive:
Our place is Ithaca; our way is home.

ca. 1942   *The Virginia Statesman*

84

Venom

Strike out in the dark and blind me,
And stifle and wound me,
And pierce my heart with your terrible sting.
I am not immune to your poison.
Nor is he.
I have no beauty to combat
The beauty of your face;
No venom to outsting the venom
Of your scarlet lips;
No fire to oppose the fire
Of your wicked eyes.
You are cruel and strong—
That slender form of yours
That seems so frail—
And he is weak,
Who seems so toweringly tall;
And I am weaker.
And you will win him because your belly
Is accustomed to the forest paths
And the thorns and the blood—
And you want *my* blood.
You will win him because your fangs
Are sure and steady
And your prey is weak.

I have no testimony to offer
Except that I hate snakes
And all things that crawl
Along in mud, fangs poised,
Ready to strike at any victim
In order to lessen their insatiable lust
For blood and tears;
No testimony except that I hate
The look in a woman's eyes
When she likens herself to a reptile.

1942

WIND

The wind is a tall, bare-headed beggar
With tattered clothes flapping in the fire-glow.
He stops before the blaze to warm his hands
But for a moment,
Then moves on, his head thrown back,
His teeth glistening in defiant laughter.
The wind knows he is an outcast;
He knows that doors are barred against him,
But he does not care.
He knows come March the world will bow
Before his beggar will.

Ivy Leaf
June 1943

ELAINE

Elaine
With the late sun on your face
And the golden clouds in your gray-green eyes.
Elaine . . . . . Elaine . . . . .
With the zephyrs in your hair
And the waning light of day in your smile.
Elaine
With the shadows gathering in your eyes.

What clouds? What shadows?
Beautiful—but sad!

Get out of the city—
Go back to your hills
Where you can run and laugh and be free.
Elaine, Elaine,
Go back and find your happiness.

ca. 1942

CONVENT HALL

Four walls, four empty, blank, and cloistral walls;
A loveless garden fresh with fruitless tears;
Illicit thinking that my mind enthralls,
Grown weary of its sacrificial years.

I sit here wordless in the twilight gloom
Damned by a smoldered fire akin to pain.
There may be silent peace within my room,
But oh, the stormy turmoil in my brain!

I have been trapped. Alas, what cruel fates
Tricked me into existence of a kind
That molds the things I do, that permeates
My mode of living, but excludes my mind?

To me I am a deathling doomed to hell.
Even the sacred shrouds I wear imply
That there are secrets I shall never tell
Until, of fear and pain of them, I die.

Nowhere but in my face do I conceal
My wistful longing for a world forsaken,
My sorrow for a cause I do not feel,
My secret joy in trees that I have shaken,

Of fruit so bitter-sweet it burnt my mouth,
Of stolen happiness like birds a-wing
Flying to meet me from their golden south
Once when the budding year was at the spring.

Ah dear, lost spring! For this year, even spring
Is not the breathless May I used to know

In days when I was free to weep and sing,
A year, a century, an age ago.

This is the substance of my sorrow:
Lover-worn, weary of passion, weary of pain,
I sought within these walls a new tomorrow
And help from turbulence and peace again.

I found them not; there is no peace from sinning,
No refuge even in this convent room.
What seemed the end is but a new beginning
Of weariness which, in itself, is doom.

But I have taken up the cross to bear.
Forever to the deaf and weary moon
I must go on and lift an empty prayer
That care may end—that death may follow soon.

ca. 1943

FROM A TRAIN

I am looking for something I know I cannot find,
But I go on searching—fool that I am!
Thus am I here.

    I seek you, but with every dawn
    I lose you, world without end.

New Orleans . . . . .
Pretty painted faces laughing—
A mixture of all the tongues man knows.
Surely, if one would learn the heart of all races,
Here would he find it.
But no, there is nothing here.

    I seek you, but at every dusk
    You are a fleeting thing.

Wide stretches of plains,
Arid, bare, before I enter another city
Walled with mystery.

Across the Mississippi, across Eads Bridge
Into a smoky city, grimed by the memories
Of many a winter.
Saint Louis . . . . .
Art Hill in Forest Park and a statue
Of the saint-king on a horse
Riding away, riding away.

    I seek you, but in every train that passes
    You are riding away.

Riding to Chicago on sleek, steel rails—
Lights, music—are they not empty, too?
I must catch me a train and get away from here!
Down in the ship yards, cargoes of everything I do not want

Headed for unknown ports,
Every one like the last port left behind.
Where to go? Where to go?

I seek you, but at every station
I lose you, world without end.

Quill and Scroll Literary Supplement
The Virginia Statesman
May 2, 1942

TO A MAN WITH WINGS
(To Wilbur F. Long)

Art thou the child who led me from all things
That were my little griefs of bygone years,
Now grown into a man with silver wings?
And art thou still, as ever, without fears?
Thou wert the second of our father's home
To come into the world and bring delight,
The first to shape great dreams, the first to roam
On raptured wings into the waiting night.
And now thou hast been granted breezes free
And cloudless skies and spaces unconfined
And to the heavens a close proximity
And soaring mind.

I love thee, brother, friend, and memory,
Though Time hath robbed us of those other years,
Shaped thee a stalwart man and made thee free
And given other lips to kiss my tears.
God give thee wings not of a silver cast;
God grant thee altitude not found in air
And happy landing in smooth fields at last:
This is my prayer.

1943   *The Virginia Statesman*
                              February 8, 1944

PRAYER FOR STRENGTH

God, give me strength to hold back idle tears;
Strength to walk through a wilderness of woe,
Though I may see no sun to light my path
And though the days in silence come and go.

Forbid my resignation to despair;
Grant me defiance of self-fashioned pain;
And though my tortured eyes long for the sun,
Help me to stand alone and face the rain.

Allow no useless words of grief to fall
From weak and trembling lips; my whole life long,
Though dawn may never interrupt my night,
My God, help me to lift my voice in song.

ca. 1942

PRAYER FOR FAITH

Help me to walk through unbelief, believing;
To pass by Reason's sanctuary blind
When reason would dispute my soul's first impulse;
To trust my heart when doubts would fill my mind.

Let me refuse to hear the idle chatter
That falleth from the unbelieving tongue;
Let me retain my love of joy and beauty
And the ethereal worlds dreamed by the young.

I dream a world; I fashion misty patterns
Of youth, of love, of deep and boundless seas.
By all the tears and laughter spent in dreaming,
Lord, never let me lose my faith in these.

ca. 1942   *The Tuskegee Institute Chapel Bulletin*
                February 21, 1943

PRAYER FOR FORGIVENESS

Lord, I have sinned in that a bitter seed
Has borne its ripened fruit within my heart,
And Hatred's house has been my mind's abode
Where I have dwelt in tears, alone, apart.

Forgive that fevered impulse of my brain
And let me calmly temper it with trust;
Let all my tears be tears of penitence
And not of ruthless hate, if weep I must.

When enemies intrude upon my peace,
Help me to face them rich with Christian living,
Then bow before thee with a contrite heart
To be forgiven and to be forgiving.

ca. 1942

UNFINISHED SONG

1.

Love came again today like gusts of spring
As fresh and vibrant as an April rain.
He spoke and nightingales began to sing;
He smiled and then—I lost my heart again.

2.

The world was dark until you came along.
No roseate dawn would break, no sun would rise,
And no unfettered thrush would lift his song
In peace and freedom up to cloudless skies.
Life held but gray, impenetrable gloom—
The beat of footsteps and the sound of rain—
The din of cities, and within my room,
The silent, stifling lull that comes with pain.
But when you came, the old world ceased to be;
You changed the skies, once dark, to cloudless blue
And you became the moon and sun to me
Because I found a whole new world in you.
My life became a never-ending song
That glad, decisive day you came along.

3.

The song I bring you will never end.
You were a whirlpool that sucked me
Into your magnetic embrace,
And it was fantastic, I know,
And mad. But I was submissive.
I could not resist the sweep of water
That stormed over my head.
I did not try to breathe;
I was content to be swallowed

And lost in the tide of your overwhelming love.

I sing because I am happy
To have you as my never-ending music.
On and on and on it will go,
This song . . . . .

4.
Nothing in this world would I withhold:
Neither sun nor showers,
Springtime fragrances, bright shining gold,
Blissful hours,

Moon or stars (if they were mine to give),
Skies of cloudless blue,
Breath of life with which I proudly live
Just for you.

All the things my fingers could ensnare
Gladly would I take,
Molding them with deep and earnest care
For your sake.

But the years and days I do not own
Or the realm above.
I must come to you poor and alone
With my love.

August 12, 1943

5.
I had been young and beauty then had been
Some glazed and shallow cup from which to sip
The too-sweet wine that blind youth glories in—
Some heady pool in which to bathe and dip.
I had not known the white wing of a dove
Could bear so deep and infinite a woe
And make it beautiful. Such pains of love
Were passions that I dreamed but did not know.
But overnight, a herald blessed my sleep;

His name was Beauty and his realm was Passion.
He said: My secrets you must learn. Oh weep
That you have found me in so bold a fashion!
And I was old; Beauty, I knew in truth,
Was not the polished surface of a cup
As I had once imagined in my youth.
The shattered fragments, as I picked them up,
Within their inner selves revealed to me
Strange wonders that before I could not see.

6.
My songs go unfinished . . . . . as you willed that they should . . . . . the
Muse comes and sits with me awhile . . . . . sharing my complaints
. . . . . for awhile . . . . . but before I can tell her all that I would
have her know . . . . . she rises and flits away like a flighty woman
. . . . . unable to retain her interest long in human affairs

My songs go unfinished . . . . . as you willed that they should . . . . . for
I pick up my pen . . . . . and wait with patient fingers . . . . . wait for
beauty to come . . . . . wait for these soft young things I feel to take
form on parchment . . . . . but the Muse becomes trite and foolish
like a gossipy woman leaning over a back board fence with her
neighbor

My songs go unfinished . . . . . as you willed that they should . . . . .
although I begin well . . . . . there is no resolve . . . . . no constancy
. . . . . for the Muse is irresolute and inconstant like an autumn
woman . . . . . ever-changing

My songs go unfinished . . . . . as you willed that they should . . . . . for I
would burden the Muse with the weight of my cares . . . . . if she
would only listen . . . . . but she is like a haggard old woman with
deep-sunken eyes . . . . . seeking to escape from ancient sins . . . . .
and my songs are young

My songs go unfinished . . . . . as you willed that they should . . . . . for
nowadays she has no time . . . . . the Muse is like a tall dreaming
woman detached from the cares of so weary a world

My songs go unfinished . . . . . as you willed that they should . . . . .
my songs would be soft and soulful . . . . . my songs would be a
young girl in her confirmation dress . . . . . but the Muse has
become a selfish hard-lipped woman who will not see beyond her
own hurts

My songs go unfinished . . . . . as you willed that they should . . . . . they
would be wistful and a little sad . . . . . and I would beseech the
Muse to weep with me . . . . . to know the piercing wounds you
make me feel . . . . . and at first she is sympathetic . . . . . then she
becomes only tolerantly patient . . . . . and in the end she is a
wanton woman with dark eyes in a hurry to barter her soul for a
gayer tune

And I wonder if . . . . . although you willed it so . . . . . your eyes also
would be distant and detached . . . . . if I came to you only with
unfinished songs . . . . . and my hands otherwise . . . . . so utterly
empty

7.
Rain
Rain and wind
And a tearful
Goodbye.
Gray skies
Overhead—
Infinity—
Eternity:
Endless months
Of loneliness
And waiting.
Gray pavement
Wet and cold

Underfoot—
Impatience—
Monotony:
Fruitless seeking
And dreamless sleep.

So you are going
And the torrents
Will bewail my loss,
And the cruel winds
Will bite into my flesh
And sear my lips
And tell me
You are
Gone.

And every rainy day
That comes
Hereafter
Will remind me
That you are far away,
And every chilling wind
Will prove
That partings
Are not kind.
And I will join
The rain
And the wind
And the somber mood
Of gray days,
Losing myself
In their despair
Until we meet again.

8.

The moments you're away are filled with pain,
For when you go, the doubts and fears leap up;
The sunshine of your smile gives way to rain,
And tears of sadness over-run my cup.
There is no peace to still my troubled mind
Those times when we're apart; the days are gray.
I seek and seek, nor can I ever find
A reassurance when you are away.
You do not know how vivid and how real
Can be this dark and loathesome loneliness—
Can be this premonition that I feel
That some day you may change and love me less.
You do not guess, each time you say goodbye,
That when you leave I close my eyes and die.

9.

When the train wheels cry in the night
And their wistful melody pains like a wound,
Remember me in your loneliness—
Remember that the train is lonely too
For the station.

When the darkness falls
And there is murky night in your heart,
Forget me not yet. Look to the dawn.

At daybreak—some daybreak—
Listen for the wheels rolling
Home.

10.

I wait, I wait an agony of time;
I stumble through the dark abyss of hell
To find no song to lull my weary brain,
No traces of the words I love so well.

The night is long; the wilderness is black;
Thus far I see before me no white moon

To break the silent dark I wander through.
I close, beseeching you to answer soon . . . . .

11.

While I was walking down that long last mile
    With you
There fell a brown and brittle leaf between
    Us two.

There fell a lonely autumn and a wild
    bird's call,
And I foresaw the painful tears that, too,
    Must fall.

I knew Time would not fly: it walked on
    Crippled feet;
The nights were cold and long; the days were
    Incomplete.

Ah, but the autumn's over and the tears
    Are past,
And we may take the peace that follows pain
    At last.

12.

I think you loved me, but I do not know;
I am not certain if your eyes held love
    Or merely kindness.
I cannot tell if what I felt for you
    Was light or blindness.
I do not know.
I cannot say that, when I woke to find
My dearly-woven dream of you had flown,
    My pure light faded,
Or if my eyes, profoundly blind, became
    Less darkly shaded.
I cannot say.

But this I know: that through the endless years
Your name will be my peace, no matter what
    Such dreams may cost me;
I shall yet hold you dearest to my heart
    Though you have lost me.
This much I know. . . . .

November 5, 1942

13.

At last dawn came, bringing with it its first glimmering, filtered ray of
    light and hope.
Out of the chaos of helplessness and loneliness and futility dawned
    my day.
Brief, it was destined to be, and I knew there would come a time when
    I would think it better to have never left the night.
But it was too late! My short, imperious day was already fast dawning,
    fast passing, and fast fading away.

What can I think of now that my day is over and the quick, vibrant
    tones and hues of good living are obscured by night?
What can I do while I lie in bed alone waiting for sleep to come but
    count sheep and wonder how many of them will jump the fence
    without being hurt?
And ask myself how many fences I have tried to jump and how many
    scars I got? And how many other people I hurt in jumping?
What can I do but lie dry-eyed and empty of the love that dawned and
    died with my day?

At last sleep will take me, and my day will become no more than a
    dream, a memory, and a sigh.
And in my sleep I shall be healed and cured and fortified for yet
    another dawn—if it should ever break . . . . .

14.
Let me forgive you and love you
Just the same
As if that past of lies had never been;
As if it were forgotten—
That mist of deceit and misunderstanding
That led us to the crossroads.
Let me forget that there was ever
Something in you of which I was ashamed;
Something that I despised;
Something that I could not understand.
Let me forget all that dark
River that surged between us
And love you just the same.

Let me forgive you and love you
For what my heart's blindness
Pictured you to be;
For what my soul's sincerity
Trusted you to be;
For what my love's undying faith
Believed you to be
And never doubted that you were.

Let me forgive you and love you
Silently, in the cloistered loneliness
Of my heart;
Love you until the walls of my being
Would expand and break;
Love you although I turn my back upon you
For my pride's and the world's sake.

Let me forgive you and love you
Just the same,
Heart, soul, and life—
No matter what the cost.
If memories are the compensation
Of dear things lost,
I will be compensated!

15.
Yes, I shall miss you.
Truly? Yes, truly.
You have always been the most true
Of all the truths I have known.
And I shall think of you.
Honest? Say 'honest.'
Honest, honest honest!
Yes, I shall think of you
More than once in every tortured day
And never ceasing through the turbulent nights.
Honest.
I shall enter the house and think:
The house where he was and will never,
Never come again.
I shall climb the hill and say:
O God! How can I forget this hill
One night in the rain!
Everywhere, everywhere I go,
You will be there with me—very!

Yes, I shall miss you.
Red of the sun, white of the falling snow,
Black of the night,
And all the cool, somber in-between shades
Of life. Yes, miss you!
And what for?
For the few fleeting hours we shared,
For the heart-breaking dearness of your voice
And the deafening silence of our silence,
For the oblivion of all the things
That existed unnoticed
Because of you,
For a future that is no longer a future
And a dream that is no longer a dream
And a song that is no longer unfinished.
It is finished—finished as it started—
Quick, impulsive, like a gust of wind,
Like a whirlwind catching me up,
Completely enveloping me for a moment,

Then casting me away,
Leaving me lying limp in the long, cool grass.
But the spell is not gone—
Not for me—honest.
Not for you either? Good.
Of course I knew.
Knew that the flame cannot die.
You knew, too,
And somewhere you will lie limp,
Too, in some cool, dark place;
Will wither your life away remembering.
Yes, I shall miss you.
Shall we meet again? No, never.
Dreams that seem real
Become only dreams upon awaking.
No, never, never dream again—
Only remember.

Ah, believe me, dearest,
It was meant like this.
I did not plan it thus;
It merely happened—who knows how?
Not I nor you.
But I shall think of you.
Honest? Say 'honest.'
Yes, I shall think of you
More than once in every tortured day
And never ceasing through the turbulent nights.
Honest.

May 13, 1943

ONE AND THE MANY

ONE AND THE MANY

For every timid dream that nestles briefly in my palm,
A thousand get away.
To each stray note of joy resolved into the harmony of song,
A million minor chords reply.

But I do not begrudge my dreams their flight,
My hopes, their wantonness,
Or my songs, their discord;
For the few that linger and are pure and true
But prove the miracle that one thing can be constant
While the many go.

NOVEMBER

And did I think the fall unbeautiful
When I was young?
And did the trees seem desolate
With color wrung
From every limb?

Ah, but I can discern
In my own afternoon
The leaves that turn and fall—
Youth's bright adornments
(Fluttering absurdities)
Grown useless, dull, and ready for the earth.

And I can see myself left straight
And clean and strong and unadorned
And do not think myself unbeautiful.

ca. 1955

QUEST

I will track you down the years,
    Down the night
Till my anguish falls away,
    Star by star,
And my heart spreads feathered* wings
    Where you are.

I will find you; never fear—
    Make you mine!
Think that you have bound me fast
    To the earth?
I will rise to sing you yet,
    Song of mirth.

I will let you think you won,
    Perfect dream,
Till I creep from dark and toil
    To your side,
Hold you to my heart and sleep,
    Satisfied.

I will track you down the sky,
    Down the blue,
Till my song becomes the sun
    Of the years
And the golden April rains
    Are my tears.

ca. 1945   *American Literature by Negro Authors*
            edited by Herman Dreer (Macmillan, 1950)

---

*"Feathered" changed to "flaming" in *Star by Star*

NIGHT WATCH

I cannot sleep, I cannot sleep,
The fires burn too bright;
The moon has slaughtered little stars
And driven clouds to flight.

I could not dream or hope to wake
If I should shut an eye;
The moon has routed meteors
And chased them down the sky—

The murderous moon with bloodshot gaze,
Inebriate, insane,
Rushing before the sun can claim
Omnipotence again.

SUMMER DAY

Here where the world is quiet and the grasses
    Wave banners in the breeze,
I sit alone as one more season passes
    In afternoons like these.

The lazy days, the days of summer splendor,
    In peace and ease are spent,
And only in my fingers, tense and slender,
    Is shown my discontent—

Small fingers closing tenderly and dearly
    Upon the pain they clutch,
Aware that what they capture is not nearly
    Enough, yet is too much.

June 14, 1951

AFTER

The doves are in the eaves
Flapping their eager wings.
And I am going.
Oh, pity the last lonely birds
That fly into the setting sun.

Shadows of their wings
Fall in purple sadness
On the cold damp sod.
Pity the last birds
After the flock has flown.

The doves are flapping impatient wings—
The late birds flying alone
And cooing a farewell
That is forever goodbye.
Oh, pity the last, still-later mortals
Who have no wings—
Who may walk in the purple shadows only—
Alone, alone in the night.

May 23, 1943   *Midland Poetry Review*
                      December 15, 1947

DREAMS

Tell the fair dreamer, now that dreams are over,
That he has lost that which was best to know.
Highways were not more peaceful to the rover,
Nor ever did the silent hills of snow
Better become the twilights of December.
Tell him to seek again the star-pale hour,
The fragile and the ever-magic ember
That warms the soul as summer does the flower.

ca. 1946

FOR ONE SO BRIEF AND LOVELY DAY

For one so brief and lovely day
Dreams were the silk my childhood spun;
Love was the flame with which one may,
With truth and courage, light the sun.

Again the faith was sure and strong
Once, for as long as dews remain;
The path of joy was broad and long;
The hope for peace was bright again.

I knew the old, lost tenderness
A thousand Junes forever sing,
The clear view trusting hearts possess,
The fountain self-replenishing.

But now my ancient, sage unrest,
My tempest-tested common sense
Remind me that the fruitless quest
Is always my experience.

And I am back to what I learned
Through disappointment, loss, dismay:
The dreams were false that I discerned
For one so brief and lovely day.

PROVERB

Believe not that all lovely things shall last,
For you shall live to know
That often where the choicest seeds are cast
The foul weeds grow.

ca. 1945   *The Michigan Chronicle*
               Between August 3 and October 12, 1946

END OF SUMMER

Beneath the green a flame of scarlet leaps;
It is the first leaf turning, turning?
Soon there will come the time of year that weeps,
With angry colors burning, burning.

Ah, heart, I told you it would have to come:
The smell of autumn smoke ascending—
The year-end passion throbbing like a drum—
The summer's melancholy ending.

But, oh, the green, fantastic spell of May
With homesick robins homeward winging
Will come again some more-than-perfect day
Where Love's proud angels will be singing!

ca. 1945

THE WORLDLING

Oh, blow me worldward, wind of my desire!
The close, the peopled hills are not my home;
The free and open spaces light a fire
Within my surging soul, and I must roam.

I would have steeples reaching to the sky;
I would have pavement, firm beneath my feet—
The earth-old call of places that are high
And broad and deep—else I am incomplete.

There must be always freedom for the free.
O crowded hills, the time has come to part.
You've done your most, your very last to me:
Farewell, my hills; farewell, my foolish heart!

ca. 1944

CITY THOUGHT

Is this my house, I ask?
Is this my fine white house in a great, wicked, sinful city,
Standing alone, fortified, barricaded against—what?
Is this my pure, white, untouched house, watchful of being
  tainted, afraid of being tainted, guarding against being
  tainted?
O my own love, my city street, gray and dirty!
O my vagrant thoughts wandering like gray pigeons on a city
  street!
My pigeons are young, but they are fearless and undaunted;
They do not mind the brown grasses that wither at October's
  breath;
They do not mind the fallen leaves that cling in damp
  puddles on the gray pavement;
They do not mind the cloak of sullen clouds that the sky
  wears,
through which, after a recent rain, a timid autumn blueness
  tries to break.
They do not mind the trees that stand stripped and pitifully
  naked in the brisk wind.
These pigeons, they fear nothing; they shrink from nothing;
  they flee from nothing, screaming.
The drive on a busy street is irritated by the pigeons; he is
  eager to go somewhere, to be by a warm fire of an
  autumn evening. He does not like the stubborn pigeons
  boldly refusing to let him pass.
My pigeons flap their wings at security and a cozy fire, and
  turn away indignantly into the busy street.
My fine white house could easily shelter them, but they will
  not have it.
They are curious little rebels digging their talons into life,
Breaking it, looking to see what is contained within the
  crushed shell; and they will not have the house.
What good is my house, then, if my thoughts will not take
  refuge in it?

What use have I for a sturdy house if my soul will not stay
    by the fire?
I ask myself, then, is it really *my* house that stands so
    serenely mocking the world?
Is it really *my* soul that keeps its undefiled windows lighted
    with so calm and patient a lamp?

October 24, 1945   *American Literature by Negro Authors*,
                          edited by Herman Dreer (Macmillan,1950)

MY OWN

I must give back to each the borrowed dreams
I worshiped with intensity and fire—
Back to the river, all its silver streams
That never flowed except in my desire;

Back to all springtime nights, their loveliness;
Back to bright April, lyric rain and mirth;
Back to a lonely hill, the wind's caress;
Its tender green, back to the thawing earth.

I must return those hours when longing burns
With tales of far, imagined wanderings
And songs of bold, victorious returns—
The golden crops of many unborn springs.

While I undo the fabled incidents,
Your heart will come and nestle in my hand,
Giving, without regard for recompense;
Asking no more but that I understand.

This is my own at last: this night of dew—
This quiet starlight hour alone with you.

August 6, 1951

SARAH STREET
(St. Louis)

Once again I float down
The enchanted streets of my town
In a gray
Foggy dream; and the gay
Honky-tonk and tin-horn rattle
Of the bars and dance halls, and the battle
Of the street
Greet
Me with nostalgia. But I know
That I will never go
Back,
For the reality is a black
Abyss.
Only this
Remains—
Only the dream retains
Its shape, its mood and hue
And is true.

But in remembering
I see the dead years blossom into spring.
Once more the scene is new,
And I view
The super three-dimension screen
Of sudden, flashing red and green
With quick excitement and intensity.
Here alone for me
The night
Is strangely full of neon splendor and delight.

Even alleys here look beautiful and fair,
Though the air
Is foul with cat-scents reeking.

I am seeking
Symphony of cloud and smoke and fog.
Can a dog
Yelping from some neighbor's backyard, shake
My love of cities? Should I wake?
Do I mean
To return to neatly-fenced and clean
White houses in a row?
No!
I was caged
And enraged
In my small New Jersey town.
Now I frown
On its shy propriety.
I am free!

Someone asks me what it means, being here,
Feeling near
To a place that masquerades as a city:
Not a pretty
Sight, this pseudo-metropole
Sprawling like a country town in a soft-coal
Haze; sultry, painted-faced,
Embraced
Like a harlot by the Mississippi, loud
With its laughter, proud
Of old memories and touchy of old pains.
It complains
And is insulted to be called The South—
With a drooping mouth,
Calls itself midwestern. What or where
It claims to be, should I care?

Being there was looking life in the face,
Taking up the race
That may never cease
For peace

Of thought; but knowing, while I ran,
How it all began,
And understanding that the quest
Was best
By far of all pursuits.
Were its fruits
Other than this one,
I was done.

But how many fitful years
Have gone by since then! How many tears!
How many loves degraded or decayed,
Promises made
And broken, reveries gone up* in smoke,
Gilded visions tarnished! I awoke
From the youthful dream I lived, long ago.
Even so,
Once again,
Now and then,
I float down enchanted ways
In a haze—
Though reality will never yearn
For return.

---

* "Gone up" was later changed to "dissolved."

LIFE

Life is but a toy that swings on a bright gold chain,
Ticking for a little while
To amuse a fascinated infant,
Until the keeper, a very old man,
Becomes tired of the game
And lets the watch run down.

To Jill

When summer comes some other year and your fair head
Rests on my bosom in an infant angel's sleep,
What shall be left to wish for? What shall be unsaid?
What dream shall haunt my slumber that I cannot keep?

Then I shall have all wisdom, for I shall have held,
Warm in my body, unseen life and fresh creation;
Fear and unspoken want forever will be quelled
And joy will reign, and power without limitation.

For life shall flow from life as Adam from the sod
Became a heart that could not die and eyes to see
The wonders of a shining world. And only God
And I will understand how such a thing can be.

1946

WHITE CROSS

Never mind if dawns refuse to waken you
Though the hills are sleepy-blue with mist;
Never weep if lovers have forsaken you,
Seeming to forget the lips they kissed.

Heavy feet may thoughtlessly tramp over you,
Never caring that you had to die;
Silver wings of war may not discover you:
Many are the crosses where you lie.

But when Time is lying in the sod with you
And the stillness is its silenced drum,
There'll be one to seek the face of God with you—
Wait for me, my dear, and I will come.

1944   *Negro Digest*
                                        April 1963

LULLABY
(For Peggy)

Close those pretty azure eyes,
  Baby girl;
Slumber songs and golden skies
  Are your world.
God gives time for innocence:
  It is brief;
There'll be time for recompense,
  Time for grief.
If you only knew the world
  You would weep . . . . .
While you can, my little girl,
  Go to sleep.

ca. 1944

MY SONG
(For Lillian Fisher)

Oh, I shall sing my song from the deep heart of me,
The world's bright magic at my fingertips;
And where the rains have fallen, shafts of sun will be,
And birds will flutter from my parted lips.
Ah, nightingales sighing!
Ah, bluebirds flying, flying, flying!

My song shall be the snowdrops, fanciful and white,
The elfin dance of nymphs that never were;
And when my music floats across the silent night,
Sleep violets will wake to spring and stir.
Ah, lovely world sighing!
Ah, soul of me flying, flying!

1944

A SON TO HIS FATHER

Oft have I thought, since I have grown and grayed,
Of childhood ways I did not walk alone,
Of manly hands that led me when I strayed
And kindly words of cheer that I have known.

Amid life's early darknesses and fears
A constant light made clear my rugged road;
Amid the gloom of youth's most anguished years
There was a voice from which enchantment flowed.

There was a voice that still in dreams is loud,
Lending its strength till all my fights were won—
A voice that urged me to be good and proud,
That in my weakness called: "Be strong, my son!"

And I have prayed that I might pass along
To sons of mine his proud nobility,
That they might, walking in my steps, be strong
In godly ways my father taught to me.

June 13, 1949

WITH OR WITHOUT YOU

With or without you I will go my destined way,
Singing the stars and heralding the dawn;
Alone or with you, I will give my dreams their say
From now on.

For it no longer matters if your silent sneer
Seeks to uproot my dauntless crop of song;
You shall be first to witness the good harvest year
Before long.

ca . 1947

No Need of Sound

Wild lions have no need to purr
Nor crawling snakes to soar,
Nor should the sea-born whale grow fur
Or birds effect a roar.

Frail souls should have no business with
The thunderous, heavy tread,
But, finding gossamer delight,
Should weave a silken thread.

The heart that has a song to bear
Must spread its feathered wings,
And if its voice is golden-fair,
Instinctively it sings.

Entreat me not harsh sounds to make
Out of a music-word:
No eye shall view a poet's heart
Although its beat is heard.

ca. 1944

Biography

She sighed beneath the stars her weary lays
And with a choking, interrupted breath,
Looked deep into the twilight of her days
And prophesied a future that was death.

She would not see (so well she knew her part)
The sun that still shone timeless in the sky,
But awaited evening with a dying heart
And blindly let the joys of day slip by.

THE LOST MUSE

I used to be a poet once, but now
My lyre is silent
And its strings are unfamiliar to my touch.

Once when I seethed with youth's indignant rage
And burned with fiercer loves than later years recall,
I strummed my chords incessantly and purely
With fresh, new phrases never heard before.

Now when I touch the strings uncertainly,
Seeking to assure my heart it has not faltered,
The tune I labor with has some familiar, tiresome ring;
The melody is stale and cold and inharmonious,
And I forsake with rue my once-articulate refrain.

Maturity has brought its compensations, I suppose:
Love's steadier flame,
A quiet calm with which to greet the days.
I have come to terms with life
And know that right and wrong are separated
Only by a fog.
I do not trust so implicitly
Nor regret so deeply
Nor laugh so quickly
Nor weep so profusely
Nor love so tenderly
Nor hate so bitterly
Nor fight so courageously
Nor surrender with so much hurt pride.

Nor do I care so much what happens
To a fallen sparrow
Or myself
Or the world.

But I do not sing.
I have no song.

IVORY TOWER*

Oh, sing no more of pretty, useless things
And weep no more for skies no longer blue;
The feathered bird that flies on lovely wings
Is not for you.

Let towers, white and gleaming in the sun,
Be but a memory of faded dreams;
Their gods are sadly leaving, one by one
(Or so it seems).

Here is a nobler shrine, a higher god
More needed, more admired, though unsung—
He suffers with the fallen of the sod
Whose heads are hung.

He works with grimy hands for those who bleed;
He gives a vision to the hopeless blind;
He fights, his pen a weapon, for the need
Of all mankind.

Oh, sing no more the once-bright similes.
Remember now the hungry, beaten throng,
The hopeless, the defeated ones—to these
You owe your song!

October 5, 1946   *The Michigan Chronicle*
                          October 12, 1946

---

*Originally titled "The Poet Deserts His Ivory Tower"

TODAY AND TOMORROW

Breathless today I run along the shore;
The wind that lifts my hair is clear and cold;
The sun is like unto a magic door
To all the things that I shall gain and hold.

Tomorrow when this turbulence is done,
I shall lie half-contented on the beach,
Staring into a waning copper sun—
A symbol of the things I could not reach.

ca. 1943   *Ivy Leaf*

AGAIN

When I do come, perhaps you will not recognize me:
Time will have had her way with you, and tired and old,
You may not care that once I was the dream you cherished
In times when harsh reality was much less bold.

You may forget that summer once was fair and fragile—
Fairer than any other June will ever say—
And pass me by on some strange street, and never utter
The words you said would live again some better day.

1945

Do Not Pass Me By

O Life, do not pass me by . . . .
   The years are growing old
   And light for me is waning;
   My blood is running cold;
   And weary of complaining,
      I fear I may lie down too soon to sleep.
O life, was I born to cry?
   May I never know
   The sweetness of forgetting?
   Everywhere I go
   I see the sun is setting—
      Still, still I have known nothing but to weep . . . .
O Life, do not pass me by!

ca. 1944

SONNET TO BYRON

Byron, I know your wild, tempestuous ways;
I understand your driven, haunted life
Doped with a futile need that robbed your days
Of faith in man, and left you only strife.
I understand your hot and fevered brow
Deep-lined with passions of inhuman sort—
Your restless feet that stood upon the prow
Of many a ship that could not find its port.
We are the bruised and beaten of our day
Who live with neither love of life nor mirth.
We are the chaff the wind must drive away
In one blind, endless search through all the earth.
I, too, perch on a clipped and helpless wing—
A bird which, since it cannot soar, must sing.

ca.1943   *The Muse of 1944*, edited by Ethel R. Forbes
            (Horizon House, 1944)

THE LOST

I am the Writer who cannot write.
I am the Poet who never sang a song.
I am the Traveler who never passed outside his own front
                    door
And the Cosmopolitan whose world is his own heart.
I am the frustrated Dreamer—
The Seed which never grew to bloom,
The unplucked Fruit,
The Cry that never left the crier's throat.
I am the universal Introvert.

My grief is the grief of indecision.
My weariness is the weariness of confusion.
My tears are the tears of disillusioned old age,
Falling in the springtime of youth.
My tragedy is the tragedy of predestined defeat without
                    struggle.

I am the harrowed and unhappy Might-Have-Been.
I am Desire that must forever escape satisfaction;
I am the Search that must always elude the rainbow's end.
I am the Eternal Regret! I am the colossal If:
If only it had come a minute sooner, a second later,
If only I had turned down a different street . . . !

I am Youth being blown up like a balloon
Brushing against a pin's prick:
In a split-second I am shattered Nothing—
Broken bubbles, pierced balloons.
I am lost, resigned Despair watching the black, swirling
                    river from a bridge—
Searching for a Lethe, screaming to forget it all—

141

Watching the river, wanting to go, afraid not to go,
But chanting to himself the what if, what if, what if of
undefeated hope.

Oh, this time let me go, let me go!
So much piles up in the brain (*so* much!)
Like old newspapers stacked in a damp basement;
Call the junk man to haul them away
And let me have peace!

December 6, 1945

TIME IS NO THIEF

Only the minutes, not the years, are ours,
And yet, Time is no thief.
(Our love is not a time-encumbered thing.)
Minutes will go
Like raindrops leaking through reluctant roofs;
But what is lost?

Ah, say not: "I have loved a little while,
A brief, uncertain day ruled by the clock;
Then she was gone." Say not this empty thing.
Though I shall go, and all the years remaining
Will brood that other lips, not ever ours again,
Must meet,
Oh, do not sigh, my love, and do not be afraid.

Earth is not ours, but we have touched and held the stars.
The perfect golden minutes slip away;
And yet,
Time is no thief!

1945

SOLITAIRE

Your hands move across the table
In a monotonous pattern of loneliness,
Each card proving that the game is lost.
It is not a present game that holds you
In a hopeless knowledge that you cannot win;
Each printed figure is a reality that your slender fingers
Move and rearrange
But can never seem to place in the right sequence.
Fool! It is not you alone who play the game.
Some other hand deals the cards,
And you cannot change the monotonous pattern
Though your helpless hands move across the table
Hour after hour.

June 25, 1945

IMPERFECTUS

Ask the March skies how constant is your joy;
Consult the changing winds and sudden rain.
Gray mists will say your heart is but a toy!
How brief love is, dark clouds will ascertain.

How brittle and how frail is happiness!
Dash it against adversity: it breaks.
Some fond dream to your eager heart caress
And hear the awful crashing sound it makes!

Did you believe your joy infallible—
Felicity, a sure and steadfast thing?
Observe how quickly now the tears will fall
And how reluctant is your heart to sing.

ca. 1945

MASQUERADE

The lie is sometimes masqueraded as the truth.
Beneath the surface of false pleasure there may lurk an evil
    core.
The heart is often wrong and cannot be depended on
To point the perfect way.

Dangerously clothed in foolish little triumphs
Are things not worth the doing,
Songs that were better left unsung.

Never trust the spurious flame
That brightly burns and gives a pretty glow.
It may be only subtle darkness walking in disguise.

ca. 1955

REPLY

I cannot swear with any certainty
That I will always feel as I do now,
Loving you with the same fierce ecstasy,
Needing the same your lips upon my brow.
Nor can I promise stars forever bright,
Or vow green leaves will never turn to gold.
I cannot see beyond this present night
To say what promises the dawn may hold.
And yet, I know my heart must follow you
High up to hilltops, low through vales of tears,
Through golden days and days of sombre hue.
And love will only deepen with the years,
Becoming sun and shadow, wind and rain,
Wine that grows mellow, bread that will sustain.

ca. 1954

THE RUT

Wind the clock and feed the cat;
Sweep the floor and go to bed.
There is never change in that
Till you're dead.

Dance and sing a weary lay;
Laugh and weep and lightly chat;
Sigh, and at the end of day
Feed the cat.

Wash a dish and go to shop;
Mend a hole and darn a sock—
Glory! will it never stop?
Wind the clock.

Dream of what can never be:
It will never come to more.
Drown thought in a thoughtless sea—
Sweep the floor.

Dream whatever dreams you will,
Set the clock for early dawn.
Life will always stand stock-still . . . .
Time goes on.

TO MELANCHOLY

Now let me put my Words to bed
And cover up each drooping head
With loving care—for they are dead.

Where Words have died, Silence shall move,
And I shall bear her gentle love
As melancholy as a dove.

She whom I cuddle now shall stir,
But I shall make my love for her
More awful than my dead loves were.

ALWAYS

If some autumn you should see,
  Out of season,
Robins in a leafless tree
  Without reason,
Blue amid a sombre sky,
  Stars in daytime—
Never doubt that it is I
  Bringing Maytime.

Never think I will not stay
  Always near you;
Sorrow need not come your way;
  Doubt will fear you.
If this love you cherished so
  Seems denied you,
Know that where your footsteps go,
  I'm beside you.

ca. 1945

HEART-BLOSSOM

First, love came timidly and full of fear—
Love, the late bud that felt its time to grow
Was past, and shuddered in December's cold.
But then, when warmer turned the ripening year,
Up from the seed my heart had dared to sow
Burst the full blossom, colorful and bold.

I care not where or how the leaves may fall
Or when the petals that I clutch may fade
And hide their perished loveliness in gloom.
I have possessed a love grown clean and tall,
Kissed by pure sunlight, strong and unafraid.
I have grown lush and warmer with its bloom.

February 15, 1950

NEW LEAF

If I ever do love again
It will be for silver and gold.
I will love a love I can hold.

If I ever conquer this pain
I will part with youth's faithless dream
And forsake the moon's useless gleam.

Love has given naught but its tears,
Burned my heart to ash in its rain.
If I ever do love again

It will be for days, not for years.
It will be for silver and gold;
I will love a love I can hold.

October 17, 1947

IF LOVE WERE ALL

Stars have their price: with silver they are bought.
If love were all, to worship at their shrine
Would be enough. But, darling, I have sought
Their golden brilliance and they are not mine.

Paupers and beggars, we, amid the gleaming
So distant that our hands can only reach;
In darkness we have lost ourselves in dreaming,
Knowing the tragedy that dreams would teach.

But, oh, what light, what rays of sudden splendour
To eager fingers through the night would fall,
Soothing the bruise that unkind gods left tender—
If the young, faithful heart in love were all!

ca. 1947

SEASONS HAVE TO PASS

The frail, warm dream lay shattered like a glass,
A thousand fragments crushed beneath your feet.
(Time is not stagnant; seasons have to pass.
Farewell, my dream, left wounded in the street!)

A cold wind blew like winter in July;
The doubtful ember sputtered in the rain.
(All lovely things must go; all dreams must die:
Not sighs nor tears can bring them back again.)

Some dreams fade like the fragrance of a rose;
Some fall and crash like fine and fragile glass;
But none can stay. The golden minute goes.
(Time is not stagnant; seasons have to pass.)

1946

NEXT SPRING

When I hear robins singing
That all relinquished things shall come again,
And when bright April's golden promise comes to bloom,
Then shall I put aside my heart's accustomed yearning
To know that soon my lover will be homeward turning.
My heart shall bid farewell the ache of winter's gloom
And say goodbye to cloudy skies and rain—
When I hear robins singing.

1945

Epitaph

The wine of life was sweet
And drink came first;
Here lies a fool who drank
But died of thirst.

RETURN

Though you are ever more and ever more returning
(Spring to a sullen sky, seed to the soil)
And though your call, a trumpet-blast of glory,
Screams over and anew across my barren sleep—

This time, as like no other, I must strip my dream
Down to its naked skeleton
And send it thus unclothed
Into the silence and into the gloom,
Shutting the shimmering expectancy,
The sound of song without.

But you will know that my remembering
Is green and sweet and silver-bright,
Though I confine my dream
To the soft, easy uncontrol of sleep.

JUVENILE SUICIDE

Life was such a big piece of candy for a little boy,
Sugar-coated with so much artificial flavor that it made him
ill.
All he had left was a pain and an empty wrapping,
And he didn't want either one.

The Michigan Chronicle
Between August 3 and October 12, 1946

158

STAR JOURNEY

Alone I tiptoe through the stars,
Precipitously steep,
Watchful lest I should wake the gods
And angels from their sleep.

Alone I climb the secret hills
Unknown to mortal feet
And stand atop a peak where you
And I can never meet.

To you who do not dream, I am
A gently tilted head,
A voice that chatters, earth-aware,
A gay mouth painted red.

You better might possess a cold
Impenetrable stone
Than woo my body while my soul
Tips through the stars alone

January 26, 1948

THE DIVORCEE

This house was gay once, once upon a time;
Its lamps burned bright and laughter shook its walls.
Its doors were wide, and many feet would climb
Its stairs to enter into welcome halls.

But there were, too, anxieties and fears
And sleepless nights that held no hope for day;
The laughter was too burdened with the tears,
And I was wise to go another way.

Now I am lonely and the house is still
And no one comes into its darkened room
Or sees the dust upon the window sill,
And no one cares, and no one shares my gloom.

And here in bitter thought I sit and weep,
Remembering when a baby used to cry;
And here I pass my nights and cannot sleep
And curse the dawn and wish that I could die.

May 6, 1951

Where Do We Go?

Where do we go, my love? Where do we go?
The silver of young trees to ash is blown;
The sun's bright gold is but a burned-out flame.
Where do we go, Love, after love has flown?

We sing but empty songs with weary voices;
With weary hearts we mourn for what has fled:
A little spark that kept our world from darkness.
Where do we go, Love, when that spark is dead?

Like driftwood drifting idly in a stream—
Like silent ghosts in a bewildered dream—
Like hearts that are not what they used to seem,
We wander, Love—where, after love has gone?

Where do we go, my love? Where do we go?
To bury love in cold, responseless sod?
Or do we weep to drown the loss we feel,
Or do we laugh? Or do we search for God?

December 2, 1943

OVER

To love, to lose, and then to find again,
Like bringing back in May the chill of fall,
Forfeits the freedom earned through winter's frost
By singing over in the brain the thrill,
The alternating seasons love has lost.
I want no part of love that has grown old,
No ember of a flame that has grown cold:
A year has passed away—and I am sold.

1942   *The Virginia Statesman*

162

Somewhere in the City

You are somewhere in the city, lost to me,
But sharing buildings, skyline, traffic signals,
Street names, rush hours, and street scenes;
Sharing unconsciously the things we do not share
By purpose any more.
And though we do not meet, and though our feet
Do not strike the same pavement at the same time,
You are mine as the city is mine.
You and the city are one.
The city cannot enclose me in its foggy arms
Without your arms, too, holding me in a loose embrace.

Somewhere in the city you are driving someone somewhere
Or telephoning, or taking a bath,
Or making love, or watching a movie, or working,
Or polishing the metal on the car you are so proud of,
Or getting sleepy over wine,
Or telling jokes, or playing a juke box in a bar.

How many times have I barely missed you
By one block or one door or a one-way street?

Somewhere you are forgetting me
And making of me nothing—
No more than the song you listen to
Or the joke you tell—
Not so much, really!

My eyes will be impassable as fog
If we should ever meet again,
As bright as street lights,
As shallow as rain, as hard as steel.
The soft soul-eyes you knew will be for you
The barren city,

The city without love or hope or mercy or desire,
Without remembrances, without nostalgia,
Without soul.
And you will not realize or understand
How often I caress you
When the downtown lights blink on
And the traffic signals change from red to green.

October 31, 1950

STANDING BY

Know that amid your darkness I am bright
And through your gloom my heart is ever fair,
As for the blind there glows a constant light
One may not see, but feels content is there.

ca. 1945

THE TIME IS NOW

What difference does it make, now that the snows are
    falling?
The* bare, dark trees have no remembrances of spring.
No flowers are blooming now; there are no bright birds
    calling,
And winter casts its spell of death on everything.

Why mourn the loss of azure Junes? Who would remember,
In these bleak days, how bright with hope the skies could
    be?
What good are golden summer dreams in mid-December?
What pleasure now holds dawn's fantastic ecstasy?

Alas, the magic hour is past for love and roses.
They did not come; they will not come. But should I weep?
The time has come to turn from every door that closes,
To turn from dreams and settle down to peaceful sleep.

Now is no time for grieving over last year's splendour.
It is of no more consequence than last year's rain.
However sweet, however beautiful and tender,
It could not last; it will not ever live again.

O perished heart, your grief will pass just with the knowing
That yesterday has vanished and the time is Now!
Who wants to keep the embers of a dead love glowing?
Who wants to sing and sigh forever anyhow?

December 9, 1950

---

*"The" later changed to "these"

166

How Shall I Face the Dawn?

How shall I face the dawn, whose restless sleep
Is tempest-torn and weighed with loss and dread?
How shall I see the sun except to weep,
Or speak, except to say that hope is dead?

I have no wish to see another day
Paled by the dream whose truth our lives deny;
I have no will to walk the barren way
Alone in darkness, living but to die.

The fates have spoken doom upon my poor
Frail dream, and darkness clouds the light.
I ask to feel the warmth and glow no more:
Let the March storm snuff out my flame tonight.

March 10, 1950

After Parting

Yes, I did suffer, though the changing seasons
Turned green to gold and gold to barren gray;
The moon did tarnish and it had its reasons,
And sullen dawn blurred into sunless day.

So well you knew me that you did not wonder
If parting would condemn me to the Pit;
You knew your words would rock the earth like thunder.
You never had a minute's doubt of it!

You knew, and yet you let the darkness take me.
Firm in your knowledge, still you went away.
Without a backward glance you could forsake me.
Without regret you tore the mirth from May.

Yet in my heart you have been pardoned fully
For I no longer question destiny.
I know you felt compelled to go as truly
As Christ did when He turned toward Calvary.

October 9, 1951

September Lament

The leaves turn brown and fall, turn brown and fall
And that is all.

One long-dead autumn it was otherwise:
Bright flamed the treetops, cloudless gleamed the skies
And love and laughter mingled in your eyes.

In other times and in another place
I looked with wonder on your tender face
And found a warmth no winter could erase.

But I have lost it since. The leafless bough
Becomes a symbol of a cancelled vow.
Once fall was beautiful and gay; but now

The ugly dying leaves turn brown and fall
And that is all.

September 21, 1948

NOT ENOUGH

After all, silly goose, your laying days are over;
There is no time in this world to wait,
Hopefully anticipating yet another golden egg.
You have been false in a false world.

No stroke of the magician's hand
Nor crystal ball
Nor midnight bell
Nor witches silhouetted against the moon
Nor cats screaming from back fences
Shall save you.
Nothing!

It is not enough to do your miracle
And then be still.
What you have done, you have done,
And that is all.
After all, silly goose, sit down!

ca. 1945

BAD PENNY

While it lasts
I am peaceful
Somewhat.
(Shutting one's eyes,
Ignoring what is death
To see,
And floating through a dream
Is peaceful
Somewhat
While it lasts.)

But then
In the Lethean dream
A trumpet screams
And I awake.
Suddenly
I cannot help but see
The never-blending,
Never-fusing
Separate black and white.

Again
The trumpet's perhaps unintentional
Interruption
Of a dream.

1945

NOT I ALONE

Because I am not just I alone,
One individual creating momentary impressions
That are soon forgotten;
Because, instead, I am an entire people,
Baffled, confused, misunderstood,
And the weight and obligation of clarity
And enlightenment are heavy on my shoulders,
I must speak and act and think
Not only for myself but for my people.

Because not riots nor revolutions can do so much
In bitter years of bloodshed and hatred
As I can do in a brief moment of being myself—
Being my best self by which I would be characterized;
Because if I fail in destroying the myth of differences—
The myths of barbarism and filth and laziness
And vulgarity and ignorance and all the contemptible
Meanings they attach to my name—
If I fail to prove them wrong in my simplest act or word,
Then books have failed and sermons have failed,
And councils for the advancement of my people have failed.

Because none of these things is so powerful a key
To the solution of the great American problem
As the appearance and conduct which I exhibit,
Not as an individual only, but as the symbol of an entire
race,
I must hold my head higher and walk straighter
And think clearer and speak more with my mind in my
words,
For the weight is heavy on my shoulders
And I cannot ignore it.

ca. 1944   *The Michigan Chronicle*
                           Between August 3 and October 12, 1946

A NEGRO IN NEW YORK

I had forgotten so much in the South,
But now I am home and the sickness comes again;
The quick ache of remembering comes again with Grand
        Station.

You think the South is cruel because of its lynchings
And the Jim-Crow trains and the abuses
And the overt prejudice.
I think the South is ignorant and blind and afraid,
Destroying what it cannot understand.
I think the South is a drooling idiot that feels someone
Tugging at his toy and is angry because he knows that he
        will lose it.
I think the South is a master who has long mistreated his dog
And is afraid the dog, tired of the lash, will bite him . . .
A master who is afraid of being asked if he really *is* the
        master, after all.

But the North knows the yes and no to everything;
It is bright-eyed, self-confident, and all-knowing
With a cruelty and a complacency and an unconcern
That Mississippi never dreamed of.

But North, there is something that you do not know.
Come with me to Richmond and I will show you
The drama that Broadway never produced;
Come with me to Atlanta and I will let you read
The story that the *Times* never printed;
Come with me to New Orleans and St. Louis and Forth
        Worth
And I will teach you the lesson you never learned in De Witt
        Clinton High.
I will put you where life will nudge you in the ribs

More intimately than has ever happened
On the Seventh Avenue Express during rush-hour.

White man, awake from your stupor and see who talks to
    you!
(I am not what you see, because you do not look closely
    enough;
You are too satisfied with a mere glance.)
Know me, not as a joke to be laughed at,
Not as a fool of no consequence to be regarded with lifted
    eyebrow,
Not as a savage to be satiated by primitive rhythms and loud
    sounds and bright colors,
Not as a thief to be distrusted,
Not as a clown to be characterized by thick lips stretched into
    a grin over white teeth.
I am all of these—just as you are all of these.
And I am none of these—just as you are none of these.

I sing a song that is neither Big Fat Mamma nor Go Down
    Moses.
If you listen, I will teach you the words,
For this is one thing that you do not know, New York.

November 17, 1945   *The Michigan Chronicle*
                           Between August 3 and October 12, 1946

174

HER STORY*

They gave me the wrong name, in the first place.
They named me Grace and expected a bright and agile
      dancer.
But some trick of the genes got mixed up in me
And instead I turned out big and black and burly.

In the second place, I fashioned the wrong dreams.
I wanted to dress like Juliet and act
Before great, appraising audiences on Broadway.
I learned more about Shakespeare than he knew about
      himself.
But, of course, all that was impossible—
"Talent, yes," they would tell me—
"But an actress must *look* the part."
So I ended up waiting on tables in Harlem
And hearing uncouth men yell at me:
"Hey, mamma, you can cancel that hamburger
And come on up to 15-B."

In the third place, I tried the wrong solution.
The stuff I drank made me deathly sick
And someone called a doctor.
Next time I'll try a gun.

---

* A revised version of this poem appears in *Star by Star*.

REFUGEE

"Say, bud, ya gotta cigarette?"
"Yeah, man; dat's *all* I got!"
"Go way; I ain't got even that.
A cigarette's a lot."

"I had a home, a wife an' kid
An' I was ridin' high;
Along came white Jim from the hill
An' said I had to die.

"He tol' da law his po' white wife
Had suffered by my gang.
When Manny came to tip me off,
He said: 'Skip town—or hang!'

"I lef' my wife, my little kid
An' Nineteen Cherry Street,
An' in da moonless Georgia night
I moved ma weary feet.

"When I remember Cherry Street,
It hurts me to da bone;
But hell! I'm here up North—alive—
Although I am alone.

"Ain't got no job, no fine blue suit,
No new ten-gallon hat.*
I only got one cigarette:
You might as well take that."

ca. 1941   *The Poetry of the Negro, 1746-1949*,
             edited by Langston Hughes and Arna Bontemps
             (Doubleday, 1949)

---

*Revised to read: "No brand new Stetson hat."

176

NEW CALVARY

The saintly congregation of Calvary Baptist Church in
　　Birmingham (white)
Hold their Sunday-morning services in a fine brick edifice
Far removed from the Negro ghetto,
And sing loudly and in holy tones about the Christ who died
On a cross long ago and in a far country.
And they sing proudly of the Christ who arose that first
　　Easter
To show the world that he is God.
The pink-cheeked, bespectacled minister frowns upon the
　　wickedness of the world,
Flaps the pages of his Bible emphatically against the wages
　　of sin,
And assures his listeners that Herod and Pilate are burning in
　　hell.
Five hundred well-dressed people gather outside to discuss
　　the merits
Of Mr. Carthy's inspiring sermon on the historical
　　crucifixion.

Joe Jones, Negro veteran who once spent eighteen months
　　in a German prison camp,
Is dragged from a bus just outside Birmingham Sunday
　　afternoon
Because he wouldn't take a seat in the rear,
And a 1956* southern American version of the crucifixion
Takes place on a more familiar Calvary
(The cemetery of the Baptist church, to be exact)
With a rope and a blowtorch replacing the outmoded cross.
Unlike the omnipotent Christ, there will be no hopeful Easter
　　for Joe Jones;
He will never rise from his shallow grave to prove a point to
　　doubting Thomases.
And the Reverend Mr. Carthy will not flap his Bible
　　emphatically next Sunday morning

---

*The year in the original version was 1946

177

To decry the wickedness of southern justice, Birmingham,
   1956 style.
His next sermon will be preached on the subject "White
   Supremacy,"
And his pious congregation, with closed eyes,
Will shout amens and hallelujahs
To the finest sermon he has ever preached.

September 21, 1946 *The Michigan Chronicle*
                    Between September 21 and October 12, 1946

MONKEY MAN

Grin, you monkey, you!
Grin and go into your senseless dance
And tip the bottle higher to your distorted mouth:
Because Gin Stevens' jazz orchestra,
Which makes five hundred a week per man,
Is coming to town Saturday night
To play one crazy hour out of your thrill-infested life;
Because Saturday night you will be paid
Your irregular ten dollars a week
Just in time to pay two-fifty plus tax
For a ticket to the big-time dance,
And rent a new suit,
And pick up your baby in a white man's taxi.
Grin, monkey!

Over your reeling head sopping with grease
The world is building your tomb;
And shackles are being laid around those unconcerned
                    ankles
Twitching with the dance.
Out of your Saturday-night good time
Is being fashioned a Sunday-morning prayer in Alabama
For white supremacy and rope for the niggers.

But Gin Stevens is coming to town,
So to hell with Sunday and God and rent
And educating the children and saving for a rainy day.
There must be whiskey to drink and new soles to wear out.
Grin, you monkey, you!

ca. 1945

179

Scorn Not My Station

Scorn not my lowly station on this earth,
Though I know naught of gold and jewelled crown,
Nor taste of wine, nor time for song of mirth,
Nor chance to pluck the fruit of ripe renown.

For I, despised of all the human race,
Am proof that things are seldom what they seem,
Having inscribed upon my dusky face
A strength of which you cannot even dream.

Phylon
January 31, 1940
Vol. VI, No. 2

TO MY COUNTRY

When you walk into the sun and its searing rays
Blind your eyes and warm your face,
Do not forget that at your back
A cold and bitter blast will chill you.

And while you feast and drink the bounteous food of gods,
Remember that a sinner in the street is dying for bread.

O America, my country, my home,
While the green grasses grow tall in your front yard
And the leafy trees bow heavy with fruit,
Keep in mind your neglected alleys
Where filth and sickness thrive.

For the sun will go down
And the food for gods will be consumed
And the forgotten weeds will grow higher and more
                    menacing;
Then what will you say to the man who would not die
In spite of you?

August 8, 1946   *The Michigan Chronicle*
                        Between August 8 and October 12, 1946

181